Circle of Love

Relationshi ... viders, and Chi ... are

Amy C. Bak ... /Petitt

Book design by Cathy Spengler Design
Cover Photography by Petronella Ytsma
Photographs by Avraham Michaeli, Amy C. Baker, Cynthia Blakeley, and
Lynn A. Manfredi/Petitt

Published by: Redleaf Press
                  a division of Resources for Child Caring
                  450 N. Syndicate, Suite 5
                  St. Paul, MN 55104

Distributed by: Gryphon House
                  Mailing Address:
                  P.O. Box 207
                  Beltsville, MD 20704-0207

Library of Congress Cataloging-in-Publication Data
Baker, Amy, C. 1941-
    Circle of love: relationships between parents, providers, and
children in family child care / by Amy C. Baker and Lynn A.
Manfredi/Petitt.
        p.   cm.
    Includes bibliographical references and index.
    ISBN 1-884834-42-6
    1. Child care services--United States. 2. Child care workers-
-United States--Psychology. 3. Child care workers--United States-
-Attitudes. I. Manfredi/Petitt, Lynn A., 1951-   . II. Title.
HQ778.63.B34   1998
362.71'2--DC21   98-4948
                                                           CIP

*To the providers who have let me into their lives
and into their hearts.*   **~ AB**

*To the ones I carry forever in my heart, especially
those who have loved me back—you know who you are!
And particularly to my daughter, Laura, who confirmed for
me that there is little difference between loving other people's
children and loving my own.*   **~ LAMP**

Acknowledgements

ALONG THE WAY, countless people have supported us in this project. First, we thank the providers and parents who shared their insights, stories, and experiences. Their thoughtful and honest comments are the backbone of this book. We appreciate Save the Children Child Care Support Center for allowing us to use the National Family Child Care Conference to conduct interviews (even before Lynn became the conference manager!).

We also express gratitude to the providers and parents who welcomed us and our cameras into their busy households and permitted us to photograph them and the children in their care. We are indebted to our photographer, Avraham Michaeli, who skillfully captured their relationships on film.

While we can't acknowledge everyone who offered insights into parent-caregiver relationships, we thank the following mentors who went out of their way to support our book: Mary Steiner Whelan, Sandy Gellert, Kay Hollestelle, Kadija Johnston, Kathie Spitzley, Amy Dombro, Hazel Osborn, Polly Greenberg, Anne Mitchell, Ellen Galinsky, Linda Eggbeer, Kathy Modigliani, Cheryl-Ann Whitehead, Cathy Clark, Nancy Berlove, Joyce Lehmann, Gretel Abad, and Kimberly Northrop.

A few people stand out in ways that are hard to categorize. Lynn gives thanks to the parents who used her family child care home services and to the Intown Family Child Care Network for years of casual dialogue and insights that helped inspire this book. Amy thanks the Satellites of Greater Rochester for their dedication to personal warmth and caring in relationships between "agency people" and providers. And she acknowledges her husband, Ken, her partner in discovering the real meaning of responsiveness and reciprocity.

It's somewhat unusual for co-authors to thank each other, but we'd like to do that as well. Francis of Assisi told his followers to travel in teams of two, allowing each to bolster the other when one forgot the mission or felt unable to continue. His advice worked for us as we struggled to bring this book into being. We have seen each other through personal growth and crisis—job changes, divorce, ailing and dying parents, hurdles in mothering, and the exhaustion that comes when life and work overwhelm personal resources. Miraculously enough, one of us was always able to bolster the other or carry the load to keep the book moving forward.

The experience of starting out as virtual strangers and gradually developing a personal working relationship has enhanced our understanding of parent-provider interactions. The book is stronger because of the deep connections and growth we've experienced as a cross-country writing team. We thank each other for being willing to explore the depths of our relationship and for not giving up, even when realities challenged us to do otherwise.

Contents

Preface

THE STARTING POINT for this book—our philosophical home base—is our conviction that children should spend a majority of their waking hours with people who care deeply about them; the younger the child, the greater the need. Children must have loving bonds with caring adults if they are to develop trusting relationships, solid self-esteem, and a readiness to receive what the world has to offer. These attachments are critical for their daily mental health, their ability to learn and perform well in school, and their capacity for making lasting commitments as adults.

Fifty years ago, the responsibility for nurturing children fell to parents, family members, and kin-like friends who were at home during the day. They were the ones who comforted the children when they were sad, celebrated their accomplishments, and offered them guidance. They loved the children, and the children loved them back.

Today, with increasing numbers of women in the workforce, many children spend their days with people who are not family members. Paid caregivers are now responsible for comforting children, recognizing their discoveries, setting limits, and celebrating their milestones. Like parents, many of these caregivers invest fully in children's lives. They care deeply, and children love them back.

Although most parents recognize their children's need to be with people who care about them, they are not always comfortable with ties that grow in child care settings. They want caregivers to love their children, but they may become nervous when love is mutual and children become attached. They sometimes fear that their own ties, which have been stretched through separation, will be weakened.

How do family child care providers bond with children in care, yet soothe these normal parental fears? How do they balance the needs of children and their own needs with the needs of parents? These questions, and caregivers' answers to them, are the heart of this book. In eighty interviews, hundreds of casual conversations, and scores of written questionnaires, we asked providers to talk about their relationships with children and their families. We asked questions such as *How do you feel about children in care? Do you feel the same way that you do about your own children? How would you describe your relationships with parents? How do you balance the business side of your relationship with friendship?*

We discussed these questions with providers (and some parents) from across the country—including California, New York, Wisconsin, Tennessee, Georgia, Colorado, Michigan, Massachusetts, Texas, and Florida—from affluent and middle class suburbs, rural small towns, and low-income urban neighborhoods. We sought representation that cut across geographic, ethnic, and economic lines.

Our interview process was very selective. We were not looking for a simple cross-section of family child care providers; we wanted to hear from experienced caregivers who were comfortable interacting with parents, committed to caring for children, and happy with their chosen work. The providers we interviewed took advantage of opportunities to learn, joined family child care associations, and attended regional and national conferences. In most cases, they were veterans of five or more years; many had cared for children for ten to fifteen years, and a few had provided care for twenty years or more. All of them took their work seriously and considered themselves to be professionals.

When we embarked on this project, we didn't expect to be surprised by our findings. Amy had been a teacher, trainer, and mentor to providers since 1987. Lynn was a family child care provider and consultant for thirteen years and had served on the board of the National Association for Family Child Care for five years. We knew the field, but the information that came out of the interviews was startling.

The feelings caregivers have for children in care and their families went well beyond expected norms. Stories about parents who cared back were legion. Time and again, friendship cut across business lines, nuclear families were extended, and children were surrounded by seamless envelopes of love. Children and families were benefiting in ways we never realized were so plentiful or so predictable.

We are eager to share our discoveries with you. *Circle of Love* is organized in the following way: Each of the first four chapters begins with a discussion of issues and assumptions, followed by stories and experiences told to us by providers and parents when they were interviewed. We asked specifically about loving other people's children (chapter 1), forming parent-caregiver relationships (chapter 2), handling special circumstances (chapter 3), and redesigning the traditional family circle (chapter 4). Although we changed the names and identifying features for the sake of confidentiality, the stories came directly from our interviews and personal experiences.

In chapter 5 you'll read about the quiet crisis of substandard care, and in chapter 6 you'll find a list of recommendations gleaned from providers, parents, and other sources. At the end of the book you will find a list of references we suggest for further reading. This section also contains the publishing information of selected reports, studies, and books mentioned in the text.

Although the word *caregiver* has a broader reference, we used the words *caregiver* and *provider* interchangeably throughout the book. Providers generally are referred to as "she," except when the speaker was a male caregiver (there are a few!). References to parents and children alternate between "he" and "she" as much as possible.

We wrote this book for you—parents, educators, and child care providers. As you read about the experiences of these high-quality child care professionals and the families they serve, you will gain greater insight, understanding, and compassion for relationships in child care. We hope their stories will challenge you to strengthen parent-caregiver partnerships in whatever setting you find yourself. They have something to teach all of us; we encourage you to read, reflect, and learn.

Amy C. Baker
Lynn A. Manfredi/Petitt
January, 1998

Chapter 1

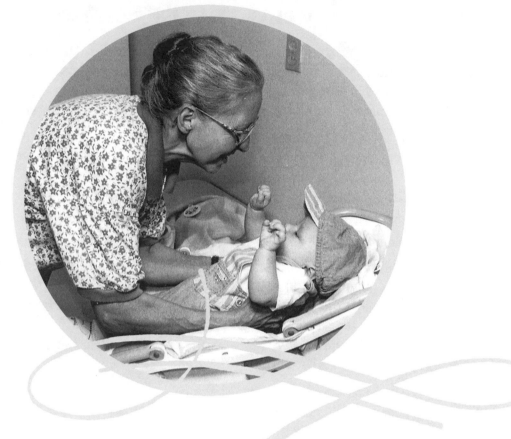

Mothering, that old-fashioned word,

is the nurturing of the human potential

of every baby to love, to trust, and

to bind himself to human partnership

in a lifetime of love.

~ **Selma Fraiberg**

Loving Other People's Children

LOVING AT LUNCHTIME ～ *"You are sopping wet, Jay-bird! Sopping! Did you know that?" Jason's mother smiles as she reaches down to lift him from the crib.*

Jason sees the happiness in her eyes and arches his back expectantly.

"You had a long nap today. I've been waiting for you to wake up for the last half hour." She lays him on his back on the changing table, smiles, and begins undoing the snaps on his sleeper. "Are you ready for something to eat?"

Jason's happy smile turns into a grimace.

"Cold hands on a warm tummy? Is that the problem? Okay. I'll be careful." Jason's mother looks into his eyes, smiles, purses her lips and makes gurgling noises in the back of her throat.

Jason listens in delight.

"Mmmmmmmm," she makes a new sound.

Pleased, Jason opens his mouth and is startled to hear his own wet gurgle. His mother smiles with joy. "What's that! You want to talk to me? What'll we talk about?" She arranges her mouth to imitate the sound Jason has just made.

Feeling her pleasure, he makes the sound again.

During the few moments it takes to complete the diapering, they gurgle and smile at each other.

"You're going to be a real talker, Jay-Jay!" she announces with pride.

Holding out her arms she asks, "Are you ready for lunch?"

Jason squirms expectantly.

"Okay. Then let's go!" His mother picks him up and holds him close to her neck. "You smell good too!" she says as she smothers him with noisy kisses.

Love Is the Goal with Young Children, Isn't It?

As a parent or caregiver, you know how important it is to have warm, intimate relationships with young children. You probably know that children learn about themselves and their relationship with the world by interacting with adults who care about them. Love and understanding grow day by day through ordinary events like the one between Jason and his mother.

In quality adult-child interactions, the adult responds to the child's needs. Jason's mother imagines his discomfort in wet diapers. Attentive to his small gestures and gurgling conversations, she notices when he recoils from her cool fingers. She celebrates his accomplishments and encourages him to extend himself because she wants the best for him. Jason's mother understands not just his physical needs for cleanliness and food, but the needs of his spirit as well—to know and express himself, to be understood, to love and be loved, to trust, and to have an effect upon the world.

Most of us would agree that the love that is growing between this baby and his mother is right and good and positive. The talking and the touching are exactly what Jason needs to become a responsive, loving child. It feels good to observe this kind of adult-child interaction.

But how would you feel if the adult was Jason's full-time child care provider? Would you have the same positive feelings? Possibly, especially if the caregiver was also a family member or friend. But what if she had only met Jason a few months ago, when his parents were shopping for child care? Would you trust the warmth you witnessed? Would it still feel right and good? What if he was your baby and in someone else's care for part of each day?

Although we know children thrive when they are part of loving circles, tradition says that these circles are not supposed to include strangers. Betty Yorburg, sociologist and author of *The Changing Family,* observes that the primary responsibility for meeting the emotional, physical, and intellectual needs of the children has always been reserved for the family group. Although this responsibility has been shared with nonfamily members, depending on circumstances, no society has ever turned over the meeting of basic personal needs to people who were not family. In the United States, in keeping with this understanding, only family members and kin-like friends are allowed inside the nuclear family circle to help raise and love the children. Love is traditionally off limits to all others, no matter how well meaning.

Historically, family-held taboos restricting interactions with outsiders made sense. They were society's way of protecting children from adults who might be a threat. Unrestrained relationships with strangers can create fears of abduction or abuse. Children can also be hurt when adults with minimal connections lose interest or drift away. Although times have changed, the taboo remains. Millions of infants, toddlers, and preschoolers spend their days with paid caregivers who start out the relationship as strangers. Many of us become uneasy with the idea that love could grow between them. We know children need plenty of love, but we are unsure; providers are outside the traditional family circle.

What do we want for our children? How should we respond when loving attachments develop between children and people who are considered to be outsiders? Should relationships like these be discouraged or avoided? Should they be discounted or ignored? Should love remain taboo outside the traditional family circle? If so, with so many children in child care, what is the cost to the individual child and to the entire society? It's time to take a closer look.

Caring for Today's Children

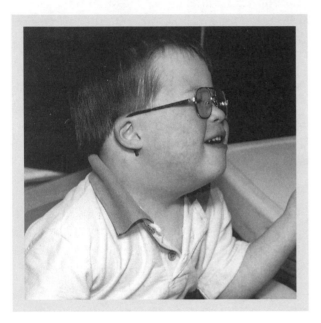

✍ **ALTHOUGH THE WAY WE CARE** for children has changed dramatically in the past thirty years, changes in the social taboos on loving and raising other people's children have not kept up. This gap contributes to the "Should mothers work?" debate, even when it is obvious that most women have little or no choice. These outworn traditions are also reflected in federal guidelines governing money allocated to states for child care. Child care block grants guarantee that parents have the right to choose caregivers for their children, even if these caregivers are unregulated, untrained, or unprofessional. (Just how *could* you regulate Aunt Bessie?)

Fifty years ago, social taboos were not in conflict with a child's need for love. Because so many mothers stayed at home to raise their young children, working parents were able to find family members, neighbors, or kin-like friends to provide child care. Most parents and providers lived close to one another and held compatible values. Bonds between children and adults formed naturally and easily. Existing ties between families and caregivers allowed love to flow freely in all directions, without concern for taboos.

In today's mobile society, family members and friends work outside the home or live too far away to provide child care. Increasing numbers of children are in the arms of professional caregivers who have no kin-like connections to families and who have values that may differ radically from those at home. Arrangements are monetary, with no guarantees that relationships between families and providers will be close. The focus is on clean, safe settings and education rather than love. Therefore, we can no longer assume that love will be a natural part of child care arrangements.

Most child care providers come into the lives of children as strangers—a position bursting with social taboos. And yet, each child's need for love has not changed. Parents who work long hours know instinctively that family relationships alone cannot meet their children's bonding needs. Therefore, they often experience feelings of anxiety and guilt.

Love Is Crucial for Healthy Development

For MANY YEARS, research in the early childhood field has supported the need for loving adult-child relationships. In 1977, Selma Fraiberg, child advocate and author of *Every Child's Birthright: In Defense of Mothering*, emphasized the important role of love and intimacy in a child's development. In her view, a person's ability to love and make ethical judgments is not determined by biology. The capacity for love is the result of early enduring human partnerships. Children who miss out on loving caretakers in their earliest years—those who have shifting or unstable attachments—grow up impaired in their capacity to love, judge, and commit themselves fully to others. The human bond can be guaranteed only by prolonged intimacy with a nurturing adult.

Heart Start: The Emotional Foundations of School Readiness, the 1992 report published by the National Center for Clinical Infant Programs, supports the same view. The infant's principal caregivers create expectations in the infant's mind and heart that affect her functioning in all developmental areas. The child who receives attention, affection, respect, and generosity will grow up feeling that others deserve such treatment as well. Similarly, a child who consistently is ignored or treated with angry, unpredictable behavior is likely to act that way routinely with others.

Despite social taboos, it is left to caregivers to bridge the gap left by working parents and ensure that children, especially infants and toddlers, are encircled with love. A smiling provider, who welcomes a waking child, teaches him what it is to be loved and feel lovable. The responsive caregiver, freeing a struggling toddler from the restraints of a stroller, teaches that child that she has an effect on the world. In a similar but opposite way, the adult caretaker who regularly reprimands or ignores a crying child teaches that child that his needs are not important and that people cannot be counted on, even if his parents are generally responsive and loving.

Research on child care emphasizes the importance of the caregiver's role when it connects quality child care and nurturing adult-child relationships. The 1994 Families and Work Institute *Study of Children in Family Child Care and Relative Care* states that parents and caregivers alike view a warm, caring, responsive relationship between the child and the provider to be one of the top three indicators of quality. Work on brain development and early child care, released by Ellen Galinsky and others in 1996 and 1997, including the Families and Work Institute's *Rethinking the Brain: New Insights into Early Development*, confirms connections between early care and brain development. Nurturing behaviors that encourage bonding are incorporated in national child care credentialing programs. National Association for Family Child Care (NAFCC) Accreditation ties research to practice when it includes some of these behaviors. In the section on interacting, they include sensitivity to an infant's body language, speaking directly to children at eye level, and respecting the spontaneous interests of each child as some of the ways to document bonding potential.

Love Is at Risk ~ Although it is clear that children need to be in deeply bonded relationships with caregivers as well as parents, the advice of early care and education experts is not consistent on this topic. While many favor nurturing relationships, most provider training promotes the more distant teacher-child or business-client styles of interaction, even with infants and toddlers, who have the most critical needs for love. Few recognize that this attitude can have serious repercussions for children who are just beginning to learn about relationships and love.

Those who do acknowledge the importance of loving relationships in the lives of children are still unsure how they should look in child care settings. Little is being done to teach practitioners how to love while maintaining "professional distance." Therefore, it is common that social taboos governing relationships between children and nonfamily members are often reinforced. As the number of children in child care grows each year, so does the potential for problems caused by a shortage of loving. The younger the child, the greater the risk.

Providers Give Hope ~ But the news is not all bad. Many caregivers develop loving relationships with children, in spite of the social taboos. They offer children high-quality, loving care, whether it is appreciated or sanctioned by others or not. "Some people think that *love* is a four-letter word in child care," observed one veteran provider who fills her home with love anyway, and teaches others to do the same.

Most of us can tell when parents care deeply about their children and their children love them back, but few can say how it should look when providers do the same. Providers who successfully love other people's children are ready to guide us through this uncharted territory. They give us hope and inspiration, building the road as they go.

What Is the Role of Love in High-Quality Provider-Child Relationships?

ALTHOUGH MODELS of loving relationships between caregivers and children have not yet hit prime-time TV, they are abundant in family child care homes. Providers abound who know how to close the gap between what comes naturally (love) and what seems safe and businesslike (distance) in order to surround children with love. Their successes show parents and other caregivers how to extend love to all children, no matter where those children spend their waking hours.

So, how do they do it? How do high-quality child care providers meet the challenge of loving for a living? How do they feel about children they are paid to care for? Do they define these feelings as love? Are they aware of societal taboos against close, loving relationships with other people's children? If so, how do parents fit into the picture? How do providers navigate the challenges that these loving relationships bring into their lives? When asked these and other questions, many were eager to share their answers.

Love Is Integral ~ For an overwhelming majority of high-quality providers, relationships with the children they care for "feel like love." Most view love as a given, an integral part of their child care programs. Parents agree, often in amazement.

"Jeanne is a treasure in my life!" volunteers a parent of a two year old in child care. "She is the only one I know who wants to talk about Keisha as much as I do. I have to hold myself back with everyone else. They think I'm bragging or competing with their children—or just a bore. But with Jeanne, it's different. I didn't understand it at first, but now I know it's because she loves my child too!"

Love Is Natural ~ High-quality child care providers are able to develop loving relationships with children who are not their own. For many, it is a source of pride. They see this inclination to love other people's children as a part of the natural order of things and can't

do their jobs any other way. When infants smile or coo, or toddlers cuddle on their laps, or preschoolers nestle in for a story, these providers smile and coo, snuggle and hug back. They are ready—committed—to being with children and doing things that other adults might consider a waste of time.

These providers sit together with children on the floor and build block towers. They go outdoors and blow bubbles when it is warm; they watch the leaves and snow and rain through a favorite window when it's not. They cheerfully play endless games of hide-and-seek or peekaboo and make snakes and pancakes with playdough. They share meals, help children settle for naps, and struggle through the complicated processes of bottle weaning, toilet training, and walking with fondness and joy.

High-quality caregivers enter into children's worlds. They feel each child's successes, fears, and failures. Like parents, they celebrate children's accomplishments, calm their anxieties, and soothe away their sadness. They do it spontaneously, with gladness and a whole heart—even though they do begin as strangers.

"You can't keep distance, and I don't know any day care mother who can!" shares a provider from New York. "You get so close to that child....If you have a child for two years, it's almost like your own....You've been with them twelve hours a day, all their waking hours...all their playing."

"It takes a while to build up the joy bond with children," writes a veteran from Georgia. "After a few months together, Cali and Katherine are as happy to see me in the morning as they are to see their parents in the afternoon. I feel the same about them."

It should be no surprise that love is the natural and predictable by-product of sharing life so fully with a child. Love is a hidden but critical element of quality child care. It may be overlooked, misread, or misunderstood by society, and even by some providers themselves; but it is felt by the children and by any of us who dare to look with our hearts.

Love Is Highly Personal ~ Although providers have no doubt that they experience love for the children they care for, they describe this love in a variety of ways. Respectful of social taboos, many downplay the emotion. When gently prodded, however, most describe this personal and private experience with honesty and great joy.

"I do love my child care children," reveals one forthright provider. "It is not the same love parents feel for their own child, but it is love. I try to provide the same nurturing for my child care children as I do for my own children."

"It depends on the age of the child and his needs," explains another. "I have stronger bonds with infants and with children with special needs. When a child enters my program who is older, and more independent, I still feel close to the child, but there is a little more distance between us."

Many caregivers agree that the strength of the tie depends on the child. Some children like to snuggle and cuddle, while others are more withdrawn and more solitary in their play. "I get close to all the children, but over the years, some children stand out more than others," muses a sensitive provider. "There's some kind of chemistry or magic that makes my relationship to them different. With those children, I feel what I feel toward my own. The love is stronger."

A provider who is also a stepparent makes different distinctions: "I match my connection to the child with the relationship she has with her parents, just as I have with my stepchildren. If I don't see a strong bond between a parent and child, I have a hard time bonding, and then I feel frustrated because I know how much the child needs to be attached to someone. I want the strongest bond to be with her parent. Otherwise, it feels unethical. I might not be in that child's life forever."

Past experiences cause some to be careful of love. "I learned from foster care to set limits to my love, so I wouldn't get my heart broken," reveals a California provider. On the other hand, experience causes others to be prepared for it. A Colorado expert tells parents in advance that she is "going to fall in love with their child and that their child will fall in love with me, and that is a good sign."

Explaining her experience visually, a provider from Tennessee draws circles around her heart. "My own children are in the innermost circle. The child care children are next, further out but still close. Other people—their parents, friends—have a place in my heart, but they are in a circle further away from the center."

One trainer describes these as "intimacy circles." She teaches providers that some children and families will have a closer relationship with a provider, and that's okay.

Occasionally providers find that they feel closer to the children they are paid to care for than to their own family members. A woman who has been providing care for twenty-two years also has a family of her own with members whose ages range from sixteen to thirty-five. "All six of my children are adopted and all are very special to me. [But] when it comes right down to it, I am closer to my day care children than I am to my grandchildren. The grandkids all live far away, and I do not see them as often as I see the day care kids. All my day care parents know that in an emergency, their children can move into my home and be a part of our family. [They] know [they'll] fit in and will be loved."

Despite variations, bonds of love are strong in the homes of these caring "strangers." Love is that subtle ingredient we all sense when we are in the presence of quality. It is what children need from their caregivers, taboo or not.

Love Can Be a Family Affair ~ Many family child care homes offer children a whole family to love. A provider in rural New York, who is the mother of teen-age children, says that when her husband comes home the babies in her care run to him and hug his knees. When he sits down to read or relax, they climb onto his lap. The teenagers enjoy the babies too. "One of them eats dinner with us every night. She's the star! If she gets corn on her forehead, we all laugh!"

"I tell the families, 'You're putting your kids here and your kids will be a part of my family,'" shares another. "This is the way I run my business."

Love can also join a provider to each of the siblings in a family. One Michigan provider has "had all three kids from one family. They were one of my first families. We've taught each other a lot over the years. They are the easiest family I have because there's been so much love shared between us. I'd say it's been a very good match for all of us. If I were to close down and they had a fourth, I believe I'd re-open to be there for them."

A mother in Georgia knows the importance of a long-term child care relationship from personal experience. "When I was little, my mom always worked. [We went to Zita's house] and she took care of all three of us. We loved her! She was just always there... and we are all still close. She came to my wedding, and she sat right up there with my mom. When I want to know about how I was when I was a baby, I call Zita. She's almost 80, but she remembers things my mom doesn't. That's what I want for my own child: someone who will be like family for all of us."

This bond of love can span several generations. It is not unusual for providers to care for the children, and occasionally grandchildren, of the children they cared for. One veteran provider tells of opening the door to find her son's long lost best friend, a boy she had cared for during infancy. He was looking for child care for his new baby. "Where else would I even consider going?" was all he had to say.

Love Is Not without Risks

~~~~~~ **BONDS BETWEEN CAREGIVERS** and children can be stronger and deeper than parents—or even providers themselves—realize. For many providers, love becomes a hidden job hazard; for children, a potential risk. Even when contact is minimal, connections of the heart can and do remain intact over time.

For some, the bonds last a lifetime, as this parent's story reveals. "I was home for my father's funeral and the house was crowded with people," she says, "I was feeling sad and disoriented until I heard a woman's voice across the room. She had her back to me in a doorway, but somehow she seemed familiar. I felt a sudden sense of well-being, that I was safe and loved and that everything would be all right. I went over to see who she was. I didn't really recognize her face when my mother introduced us, but I understood why she had that effect on me. She was my child care provider from when I was a baby! I hadn't seen her since I was four."

Although most of us assume that children who go to child care usually lose contact with their providers over the years, many do not. Sensing the importance of these connections, high-quality providers often hold yearly reunions; many send birthday and holiday greetings; some maintain social connections over the years. Shelves of photo albums, recent pictures on the refrigerator, and mementos of children once cared for are predictable features of most family child care homes. "You carry them with you. You don't know where they are after they leave you, on weekends or at night....When they move on, you carry them with you."

Children reach out to former providers too. They ask to send letters or drawings, call on the phone, or make spontaneous visits long after child care relationships have ended. Parents report in amazement that providers are remembered for years in children's prayers and are often first on their lists for invitations to recitals, bat or bar mitzvahs, confirmations, graduations, and even weddings.

When parents do not value the bonds between children and caregivers, however, they can lose touch with one another forever. Grief is a typical response on both sides. This emotion can be a huge problem in a society that considers love between children and caregivers to be inappropriate in the first place. Many providers have a hard time admitting to parents that they grieve over children who leave. Aware of the taboo, they are reluctant to voice their feelings about losing children. Those who dare to speak risk revealing their anger—and their love.

Separations can be painful, especially if a provider has cared for a child for several years. "Parents think it's bad when their first child gets on the school bus," says a provider who recently suffered the loss of a child who was close. "They ought to try this! Have parents ever thought how it feels [to providers] when their children leave?"

At a national family child care conference workshop on grieving, caregivers learned strategies for coping with their feelings by analyzing different loss situations and composing farewell letters to children they had trouble letting go. One provider was so overcome

she had to leave the session. She had never allowed herself to admit the depth of pain she was still carrying after a year of separation from a child she had loved and lost.

The pain is deeper when a parent moves a child without warning. Parents sometimes decide spontaneously to move children to grandma's or a friend's home down the street to get care that is cheaper or more convenient. The consequences to children and providers are not always considered. When the move is the result of conflict between the provider and the parent, feelings of loss and guilt are worse; however, even when caregivers anticipate separations and accept them as natural—when a family moves out of town or a child graduates to kindergarten—they still grieve. Many retire favorite toys and cups or never use special nap spots again. Some do this unconsciously, not seeing it as a sign of lost love. Others cope intentionally with the loss and allow time to pass before replacing children who have gone. When the coping becomes too much, more than a few close their businesses and look for "easier" jobs.

To reduce grief-related burnout, a caregiver in California talks to parents in advance about her feelings. "I tell them I go through predictable stages of grieving: denial, anger, loss, acceptance. I let them know that because we've become very close, I'm going to be feeling these things when their child leaves. Sometimes, parents who are taking children out of my program come to me, surprised, and say they are feeling the same things, and we talk about it. Talking doesn't get rid of the pain, but it gets rid of a lot of misunderstandings and confusion, and that way, it's easier."

Children suffer from separation too. Although parents are less likely to anticipate their children's grief or loss, most take an active role if they see that their children are having trouble separating. "When we moved out of Lilah's neighborhood, my [five-year-old] daughter was devastated. She had been going to Lilah's since she was two years old, and she cried and cried. We still see Lilah, and she and my daughter talk on the phone; but it has been very hard."

Parents who respect and support the love shared between children and their child care providers take extra steps to maintain contact. They arrange for phone calls with the caregiver, help children visit, invite caregivers to events, and send cards or notes until the child has made a successful transition. Sensitive parents also make it possible for their children to attend reunions and keep in touch with loving caregivers over time. Like Zita's child care family, when everyone understands how to share the love, the benefits more than outweigh the risks.

Providers and Social Taboos

HIGH-QUALITY PROVIDERS are familiar with the traditions surrounding family life and the taboos against loving and raising other people's children. Most understand the confusion mothers feel when toddlers call their caregivers "Mommy." Some know the hurt of losing children when parents can't share the love and move to less intimate settings.

Generally, providers deal with the challenges of loving relationships in one of three ways (with plenty of overlap). They deny, limit, or even hide the love they feel for children. They adopt a role such as "Grandma" or "Auntie," which traditionally allows for love bonds with children. Or they approach the subject honestly and directly with parents—usually during initial interviews.

Love with Limits ~ Those who limit their love often see themselves in the role of teacher, social worker, nurse, or even baby-sitter. Many have held similar roles in the past and the role-based boundaries feel comfortable and "right." When talking with other providers, they usually call a halt to conversations on love and share their own sensible limits—especially if they have learned them the hard way. "I used to get so wrapped up in these children!" says one matter-of-fact provider to a group of fellow providers. "But I learned—and you'll learn too....You can't give your heart away like that. I learned it when I was a teacher. You [have to] keep yourself more distant."

Some providers are better at this approach than others. To those who grew up in families where hugging, kissing, and touching were reserved for intimates, distance seems natural. Others claim to have emotional distance, but the glow on their faces gives them away when they share stories about children who are exempt from their strict rules about loving. They manage to hide the love they feel, even from themselves, until they start to tell stories about "my kids."

Some providers hide their feelings from everyone but the children. They confuse loving behavior with being unprofessional and are embarrassed if they let the love bond slip out. For example, in one home, during a validator's visit for NAFCC accreditation, the nervous provider was distant and demanding with the children, and yet apologized more than once to the validator for "indulging" them when she let down her guard. Her true feelings were revealed when she settled the children into their nap routine and the validator moved herself out of sight. Thinking she wasn't being observed, the provider relaxed into a heart-felt lullaby and whispered quiet endearments into each child's ear as she rubbed each one's back. The memory still brings tears to the validator's eyes. Her story reminds us that, since providers usually work alone, the children may be the only ones who ever really know the depths of their caregiver's love.

Hiding their feelings from parents is another common approach providers take toward the social taboo against loving the children of strangers. For some, this is easy and practical. "I just don't let them know," quips a Georgia provider, simply and honestly. For others, it requires more thought and individual decision.

"When parents accept that a child can love more than one person, there's no taboo about hugging their children," says one provider. "But when parents can't share, I keep the hugging times to the day. When they come for pick-up, I give their kids a quick kiss good-bye and leave it at that. They never know how much I love their children."

"Parents' personalities affect my ability to be open about the loving bond," agrees another provider. "Some are threatened by it, so I hide it."

The decision about whether or not to keep feelings under wraps is a complex and sensitive internal struggle. Often it is inspired by a deep concern for parents, as this caregiver from California explains. "I'm not comfortable with showing parents how strongly I feel about their children because I think it would make them feel the pain of their separation more keenly. They already have enough to cope with when they work full time. I wouldn't want them to have to cope with more losses than they do."

Love with Roles ~ While some providers set limits or conceal their love, for many this is not an option. The secrecy feels dishonest and unfair, something like adultery. Worst of all, it teaches children that love is something to hide. Those who want love to be open often develop comfortable relationships with families by giving themselves roles, or accepting roles assigned by the parents. They become "Grandma" or "Auntie Lou." Most adults in the United States understand how to share a child with someone who is defined loosely as a relative; people traditionally adopt each other into family circles by using these terms of endearment. Roles can clarify the rules about loving for everyone involved.

Providers who work with teenage mothers or new parents are especially prone to this kind of role-based relationship. It is also typical when the parents are less experienced than the provider, even if the parent is older. "I'm like a grandmother," shared a twenty something provider with amazement. "I'm all ages—I don't know what age I am—but I relate to the parents like I'm a grandmother!"

Caregivers and families who accept traditional love-based roles and all that they entail generally see the match as a good one. One provider is so clear about her role as "Auntie Jo" that she teaches the children to call her husband "Uncle Jess." Her own mother, who lives with them, is the grandest "grandmother" of all. The families served by this provider get together regularly at Jo's house for meals, and some, who live far away from their biological families, celebrate birthdays and holidays with her.

"We're like an extended family!" proclaim these providers. There is a negative side to this approach, however. Everyone understands "family" differently. Providers who are clear and flexible do fine. Those who are less aware of possible variations can be caught off guard by family demands or lack of appreciation when the idea of "family" is taken too far, or not far enough. But, for better or worse, many providers swear by traditional roles that allow love to flow freely toward the children of virtual strangers and back again. They offer everyone involved a high level of comfort with minimal confusion or discussion.

Love with Honesty ~ Although it is still a bit unusual, some experienced caregivers prefer having the subject of love addressed completely and honestly. They see the creation of relationships in a family child care home as a complex and complicated process. Rather than compete with parents for love, they view their role in children's lives as complementary and collaborative, a difficult but rewarding adventure in teamwork. Helping parents understand how to share the love of their children is seen as one of their most important jobs.

In most cases, honesty and openness have clear payoffs. Providers who are intentional in their approach to love talk to parents about their style early in the relationship. Parents know what they are getting into in advance, and most don't enroll their children unless they feel it will be a good match. Many of these providers have already thought through most of the issues of loving and raising other people's children. They have developed policies that prepare parents to deal constructively with predictable problems such as jealousy, differences in values, and balancing power.

The process may vary from family to family, but the result is usually the same: an appropriately loving relationship with each child that is encouraged and appreciated by that child's parents. "It takes a while to let a parent know about the bond I have with their children. People who are parents for the first time are harder," reflects one provider who values the honest approach.

Another, who leans more toward the limited teacher-child model, with a little role-based love stirred in for good measure, agreed to care for an infant for four weeks. Wishing to experiment, she mentioned the subject of bonding during her first meeting with the baby's mother, because of a workshop she had attended on this subject.

"I never thought I would have a problem with this," marveled the mother in the interview, "but I have a hard time even sharing the baby with my own mother!" Thus began a long series of conversations and revelations between the provider and the mother about sharing the love of a child. Because of the provider's fascination with the topic and the mother's willingness to explore her feelings out loud, the love that grew between the caregiver and the baby felt natural and comfortable to all three of them. By the end of the month, the provider and the mother were amazed by the bonds that had developed in such a short time. It was clear that their discussions had made it possible for everyone to bridge the impractical abyss of short-lived connections.

One year later, this mother called the same provider for unexpected emergency child care. She thought the bond had been real enough to stand the test of time, and it seemed the least traumatic option for her child. It was amazing to both adults how easy it was to reconnect, even though the child was at the separation-anxiety stage with others. A trying situation was made easy for both mother and child, thanks to an honest approach to bonding.

Providers Are Gifted at Loving

HIGH-QUALITY FAMILY CHILD CARE providers are gifted in what psychologist Howard Gardner, in *Frames of Mind: The Theory of Multiple Intelligences*, calls "interpersonal" and "intrapersonal" intelligence. This means that they have a keen understanding of relationships with others, along with a deep knowledge of self. These gifts create an ability to value "hanging out" with children who are not their own, meeting their needs and opening their

hearts in love, knowing it will not be for life. They do for strangers what some parents have trouble doing for their own. They bond easily and with joy—and it has nothing to do with the amount of money they get for their services.

High-quality caregivers are "people" people. They have an abundance of nurturing energy, yet seem unaware that they possess any special talents. Most of us know people like this—lovers of life who choose to spend their days surrounded by children, pets, and other living things. They are the ones we flock to when we need to feel safe, comfortable, and loved. They are the scout leaders, the cookie-bringers, the nursery-workers, the party throwers, the lay ministers, and the Sunday school teachers. They sing in choirs, cultivate gardens, and grow scores of violets on their windowsills.

These natural nurturers remember to bring meals to new mothers and to check on elderly neighbors as easily as others breathe. They send birthday cards to acquaintances and bring the best food to potlucks. When we feel guilty that we aren't doing something—anything—for those in need, they are already on the scene, worrying that they aren't doing enough. It is no accident that these earth-bound angels have found their way into the child care profession.

High-quality providers are able to develop an authentic caring relationship with each child in the group naturally and with relative ease. As Richard Paul notes, high-quality providers make it possible for child care to be a "viable, rich place for learning about the very complicated, very worthwhile...remarkable world of human relationships" ("Infants in Day Care," 27). Children who are lucky enough to have this kind of care are enriched daily from their providers' natural springs of loving energy.

Because society in the United States focuses most of its appreciation on those gifted in science, mathematics, the arts, and physical agility, the more subtle gifts of relationship-building are often

disregarded or ignored. Most people—parents, early childhood professionals, and providers included—do not fully value the work of a provider. Many think that "just about anyone" can care for children. They couldn't be more wrong!

If the job were simply a matter of performing a number of custodial tasks (as the low pay often implies), they might have a point. But high-quality child care includes something more, something beyond the norm, something extraordinary. The primary job in high-quality child care is to offer unconditional love to other people's children, and not "just anyone" can do that.

Love and Quality Care ~ In an article entitled, "Who Cares for the Children?" noted author Urie Bronfenner writes, "Children need people in order to become human....The isolation of children from [caring] adults threatens simultaneously the growth of the individual and the survival of society" (142–143). Recognized or not, love is the essence of high-quality child care.

With the growing number of working parents, providers who bond with other people's children are a gift to everyone. Whether the ties are limited, role-based, or honestly approached, they provide a grounding in unconditional love that helps children grow into constructive adults, able to pass love on when it is their turn. Loving caregivers establish a foundation for mental health that cannot be reproduced in later years.

Parents who want the best for their children appreciate the security and sense of well-being that caregiver-child attachments bring into their children's lives. They let their children know that the bonds they share with their providers are authentic and valued. Even when child care arrangements are over, they help children to stay in touch.

Providers who strive for quality care welcome this support. They know that their ability to form and sustain relationships with children depends on the parents. Many reach out and invite parents into their circles of love. Others strive to develop teamwork and collaborative partnerships. Whether these relationships come easily and naturally or demand effort and time, experienced providers don't give up. They know that it is the connections between adults that allow high-quality loving child care to grow and blossom.

Chapter 2

We view relationships not simply

as a warm, protective backdrop

or blanket but as a coming together

of elements interacting dynamically

toward a common purpose.

~ Loris Malaguzzi

Parent-Provider Relationships

SUGAR BITES ✐ *"Whaaaa!" shrieked six-month-old Bethany, a large welt forming on her cheek. Three-year-old Reggie backed away, looking frightened and bewildered, as the children's caregiver rushed over to comfort the baby.*

"Reggie! What is going on? That's the second time you bit Beth today!" Audrey made certain Bethany was out of the boy's reach, and then struggled to control her anger and frustration as she debated about how to deal with Reggie and what say to his mother about this unexpected turn of events.

"This just isn't like Reggie," she assured Gloria at pick-up time. "You know how much he loves little Bethy. And he didn't seem angry when he did it. In fact, he was smiling and cooing and saying sweet things to her just before he bit her. He seemed just as surprised and upset as I was by her screams. I couldn't believe he did it twice! Of course, I didn't let him near her again after that second bite. But I just can't figure it out."

Audrey let her voice trail off. She hesitated, forming a gentle smile and trying to put a light touch to the question she knew she must ask. "I'm not trying to be nosy or anything but, you know..." She paused and started again. "I need to know, is anything going on at home that could be causing Reggie to act this way?" She wondered if she had managed to sound as concerned but nonjudgmental as she felt. She saw Gloria as a good mother and a friend. She knew how sensitive Gloria was where Reggie was concerned.

Gloria mirrored Audrey's smile, but it was obvious that she was struggling to keep her reaction under control. Silently, and at top speed, she sorted through her fears and defenses. "Is my child turning into a little animal? What did Audrey mean 'is there trouble at home'? She knows I'm a single mother! What does she expect? Is Audrey trying to blame me? How can I control Reggie if I'm not even around? Is Reggie going to have to leave Audrey's child care?" Gloria's head started to spin. The very idea of leaving Audrey's nearly overwhelmed her.

"What am I going to do?" she screamed silently. "Hold on, girl!" demanded her sensible side, as she struggled to pull back from a full-blown panic attack. "Audrey loves Reggie. She wasn't even suggesting that we leave." She forced herself to think of the problems she and Audrey had worked through together: separation anxiety, chronic diarrhea, the divorce, late payments. They'd figure out how to deal with this biting too. Her smile became relaxed as she finally trusted her voice to say aloud, "I don't know what it could be; everything really is fine at home."

Feeling secure in the relationship that they had built during two years of child care, the women began to explore possible causes of Reggie's behavior, based on things that make other children bite. Stumped, they agreed to watch Reggie carefully and to keep on talking.

Gloria called out to Reggie who had been happily immersed in "Barney." "Come on, Sweetie, it's time to go home and see Grandma. You know how much she likes to get her baby boy's sugar.

"Sugar! Sugar! That's it!" Gloria said excitedly. "Audrey, that's it! The 'sugar'! Reggie's grandmother is here on a business trip and she keeps nibbling on his cheek and saying that he's 'sweet like sugar'! That's what he's been trying to do with Bethy!"

"Ahh!" smiled Audrey as the light of understanding spread across her face. She'd never heard of such a thing before, but it fit. "Thanks! That does sound like

the puzzle piece we were missing. Now we know what to do. It's a good thing we kept talking. I never would have guessed that one."

"I'll talk to my momma," promised Gloria, feeling giddy with relief. Her son wasn't a monster after all, just a poor mimic. Wait until Momma hears about the trouble she caused!

Child Care vs. Other Service Industries

 hen you pick up dry cleaning or make a bank deposit, you don't normally tell the person behind the counter about your personal life. Mentioning visitors from out of town or an all-night fight with your spouse doesn't improve the service. In fact, it usually slows things down. Most service-customer relations are expected to be formal and limited to the task at hand.

The business of child care is different. Child care providers need to know about family life, especially when it has an impact on the well-being of children. The quality of service depends on it. Children draw caregivers into the privacy of their family circles whether they want to be there or not. Changes in the family—when Grandma visits, Mom changes jobs, or an older brother is sick— affect the way a child acts. Children use behavior to work out excitement, trauma, or stress. Depending on the situation, they may be more boisterous, more aggressive, or more withdrawn. They may revert to behavior they'd outgrown—wetting, whining, clinging, or baby talk. Personal information enables caregivers to understand behavioral changes in children and respond to them constructively.

Societal traditions can make it difficult for parents to go beyond formality and share the intimate information that caregivers need. Most families prefer to keep personal lives private. Providers feel reluctant to pry, even when a child's behavior makes it obvious that something has changed. But when interactions are formal or infrequent, providers are left to interpret children's behavior without the full picture. Trying not to "bother" busy working parents, they can jump to inaccurate conclusions that can do more harm than good. Sometimes, as with little Reggie, only the parent knows whether a child is being playful or testing limits.

Traditional ideas about public service make the parent-caregiver relationship confusing. The business model leads many of us to believe that child care is a simple exchange of a fee for services: a safe, healthy environment, nutritious food, clean diapers, age-appropriate materials and activities, and adult supervision. We assume that interactions should be distant and restrained. The elementary school model, with its boundaries between home and the classroom, leads us to expect minimal contact between parents and caregivers as well. Interaction is limited to exchanges of information about the children. Although most early childhood education encourages and supports positive relationships between parents and caregivers, these two models are typically the ones held up to providers in training. Instructors warn providers not to get too close. "Friendship creates problems!"

The family model needs to be added to the mix. As in families, adult exchanges in the quality child care setting must be inclusive, intimate, and flexible. Sharing must include such things as birthday parties, visiting grandparents, remodeling, pregnancy, divorce, and illness, because family happenings like these have an impact on young children's lives. Parents and caregivers must become partners on a team, with authentic relationships that are open, honest, direct, and respectful. Daily interaction is essential if caregivers are to understand individual children and provide the love and nurturing they require.

Child Care Arrangements Aren't Made in Heaven

THE DEMANDS ON THE PARENT-caregiver relationship are similar to demands on couples with young children. Whether the adults are bonded in love or have just met, sharing the caring can be a complicated undertaking. In a single month, dozens of situations can arise that demand value judgments and cooperation. When are toddlers ready to learn to use the potty? Should they begin at nine months, or should they wait until they're three? Do you laugh or punish when a two year old says no to everything that is asked of her? If a preschooler breaks something at the caregiver's house because he is running instead of walking, who pays the repair bill? Children are experts at bringing emotionally charged conflicts into the lives of adults who are trying to raise them together.

Although parents hope to be comfortable with their children's caregivers, most child care decisions are made quickly and intuitively—under pressure. Good child care settings are hard to find, many have waiting lists, and the best ones don't always advertise. Parents feel they have little choice because of the scarcity of available options. Providers are also reluctant to be too picky, fearing they will lose needed income. Neither group is skilled at judging the other. Good matches are not always obvious at first, and many parents and providers are unaware that their attitudes toward children are not universal.

It isn't easy to overcome these obstacles. Discussing values and philosophies at a first interview can feel like grilling a potential spouse on a first date. Our natural reluctance to ask pointed questions or to identify differences in style is compounded by social taboos that insist that parent-caregiver relationships be distant and businesslike. As often as not, adults enter into child care arrangements because they "feel good" about one another, only to discover that they have opposing values and philosophies when it comes to child-rearing.

If husbands and wives who are bonded in love have difficulty navigating these rough waters, it should be no surprise that parents and caregivers, who begin this job-share arrangement as strangers, have problems as well. Given all the challenges, it's a wonder anybody succeeds!

Traditional Attitudes Toward Women Create Obstacles

TRADITIONAL ATTITUDES TOWARD WOMEN and families compound the difficulties parents and caregivers have with one another. A generation ago, most people believed that a mother's primary job was to stay at home and raise her children. Although women have entered the workforce in great numbers, our view of the mother's role has not changed significantly. Despite the fact that today's families are unstable, that women are at risk without a profession, and that most families need two wage earners to survive, every working woman wonders whether she is doing the right thing when she leaves her child in the care of another. The image of the "perfect mother," who is at home baking cookies and caring for her children full time, haunts us all.

Even women who work outside the home by choice feel guilty about child care, especially when their children have bad days. No matter how they feel about their jobs or their careers, most mothers feel responsible when their children are tired and cranky or have trouble separating. They grieve and feel torn apart when their children are unhappy.

Women who stay at home and provide child care often have equally strong feelings about women's roles. Out of touch with the new realities of our society, many feel that mothers who work outside the home are "deserting" their young. They are unsympathetic when mothers display a lack of parenting skills or arrive preoccupied and exhausted at pick-up time. They believe that working mothers have misplaced their priorities, making material acquisitions more important than family life. Offering child care is their way of "saving these poor abandoned children."

Judgmental attitudes create a downward spiral, which increases distance. Feeling justified in their judgments, providers view themselves as saviors and become caretakers instead of caregivers. This insensitivity increases parental guilt and reinforces the mothers' worst self-images. Mothers act to protect themselves from pain by becoming busier and more emotionally removed from their children.

Finding themselves in slippery new roles, mothers and providers also turn against themselves for following the paths they have chosen. Unhappy mothers think caregivers are right and responsible for staying at home with children, and view themselves as negligent and unfeeling for going out to work. Conflicted providers judge themselves to be incompetent and lazy because they spend the day at home in T-shirts and sneakers. In this time of extreme social change, it can be difficult to support one another and remember that parents often have no choices; that life can feel thankless no matter how you arrange it, especially when young children are involved; that adults are doing the best they can as they navigate these critical social changes; and that these problems reflect societal confusion about "women's work," which will probably take decades to resolve.

Strong Relationships Are Possible

IN SPITE OF HIGH CAREGIVER TURNOVER RATES (more than 40 percent), some providers stay in business for decades, long enough to anticipate predictable difficulties with parents and develop close working relationships with them. Most of us know at least one parent and provider who ended up as deeply respectful partners in child-rearing, perhaps even as friends. There are satisfied parents who entrust their children to one special caregiver from infancy until school age, for as many as five years of continuous relationship. Some families choose the same dedicated child care provider each time a sibling is born, extending their relationships five years, ten years, and more. These adults prove strong parent-provider relationships are possible. The parents are satisfied, providers feel supported, and children are happy and content.

What Do Satisfying Parent-Provider Relationships Look Like?

ALL ACROSS THE COUNTRY, many parents and caregivers work together to create quality care for children. What do their relationships look like? How do they get started? What do they do when they run into conflicts? Do they go beyond the traditional fee-for-service model, and if they do, what do their interactions look like? Do these relationships contain common elements that others can duplicate? Do the participants see the connection between the quality of parent-caregiver relationships and the quality of care? The answers to these questions echoed one another from interview to interview.

Begin with a Good Match ~ Before two people can function smoothly as a team, they have to share a common vision—similar values, style, and philosophy. Without a good match, efforts to create collaborative relationships rarely bear fruit. Many parents and caregivers learn this the hard way, through trial and error. Good matches can take many, many different forms.

"I chased my first caregiver all over the place trying to make her my friend," confesses a talkative parent from Colorado. "She was reserved and thought I wanted too much from this business arrangement. Eventually, I found a provider who was more like me. We were all much happier when I switched to her program. She and I have dinner every week or so. We take each other's kids over night and talk about a lot more than child care."

Diversity—differences in personalities, approaches, and interaction style—is part of the appeal of family child care. According to the Children's Foundation's 1996 *Family Child Care Licensing Study*, the profession includes more than 300,000 registered providers and an estimated million who are not. Each provider services a minimum of three parents. This translates into thousands and thousands of individual expectations, styles, and philosophies of care, most of which are considered "right" by some family or cultural group.

"I tell my parents we're co-parenting," says a provider who aims for consistency between child care and home, as well as recognition for her role in the family circle. "Not all parents go for it. It's not a permanent arrangement, but while their kids are with me, I expect lots of respect for my role as co-parent in each child's life."

This approach works for her, but it isn't for everyone. A father who sees it differently believes that "some information simply can't be shared with a caregiver." This parent, who is more traditional, views questions about family life as an intrusion into his privacy.

Rather than struggle over who is right and who is wrong, high-quality providers agree that it is more important to make good matches than it is to suffer through years of conflict and tug-of-war. Those who start out with some appreciation of the importance of the parent-caregiver relationship generally begin on solid footing. They tend to be able to make better matches, strengthen the matches they have, and disengage quickly from arrangements that are mired in conflict.

Since most parents lack experience in this area, it is usually the providers who take on the challenge of identifying potential matches. Experienced providers know what works for them. They have learned through years of trial and error to choose parents with compatible worldviews and expectations. They are able to state their views clearly and can gently redirect those who seem to be a poor fit.

Many providers use initial interviews to screen out families with conflicting attitudes or philosophy of care. A California provider "interview[s] parents just like they interview me. My contracts are very clear, and some parents don't call back after they read them and talk with me. That's what I want. It's hard enough getting along with parents who agree with my values."

Clarity and honesty permit parents and caregivers to identify matches—and mismatches—before the children are involved. Caregivers and parents who understand their own relational needs and boundaries are generally able to be clear with one another from the beginning. In matches that endure, each person respects the limits and expectations of the other.

A male provider from the West Coast reports: "Some people won't call me because I am a man. My attitude is that what I have to offer is a loving, nurturing role model, and I happen to be a male, which is unique." Most parents know whether they would be comfortable with a male provider or not. Other issues are not as clear-cut.

Attitudes Mesh Smoothly ~ The potential for conflict in parent-caregiver relationships is enormous. Some people think children should drink from bottles until they give them up themselves; some believe in weaning by eighteen months or sooner. Some love pacifiers; others despise them. One rocks children to sleep; another lays them down and expects them to drop off on their own. Some people want to chat at pick-up time; others hate it. Some are comfortable with drop-in visits anytime; others feel it is hard on the children to see parents come and go. Clothing, napping schedules, toilet training, and new foods all can spell trouble if there are strong differences between parents and providers.

To make matters even more challenging, parents don't always know what it is they are looking for. A mother from the Philippines who had lived in the United States more than a decade says she considered importing a nanny for her infant when she was at a loss in finding a good match. "I couldn't even say what I wanted. It was something I had had as a child before I had any words to describe it. I knew I had finally found it with Maria, even though she isn't Filipino. She holds Kim a lot, caters to him a lot, and her voice is full of joy when she talks about him. I don't know what it is exactly, but I feel at home with her."

Whether parents know what they are looking for or not, most know when they have found the right match. Attitudes toward child-rearing mesh smoothly; differences can be discussed; developmental hurdles can be met; and boundaries can be crossed with a sense of humor. Overall, the relationship is a source of comfort and relief.

Common Elements of Satisfying Parent-Provider Relationships

ALTHOUGH PARENT-CAREGIVER RELATIONSHIPS may vary in philosophy or style, all successful and satisfying partnerships have common threads. First, everyone starts with a level playing field. Parents and caregivers regard both roles as valuable in a child's life; the child's place in the family is as important as the one held in the life of the provider. Adults work to collaborate rather than compete with one another. Conflicts are seen as normal, and the focus is on problem-solving rather than establishing blame. In most cases, everyone agrees to be guided by professional policies and standards set by the provider.

Mutual Respect and Acceptance ~ Good parent-provider relationships are based on mutuality, acceptance, and respect. Adults view one another as equals, people who are important to a child in different but complementary ways. There is responsiveness, authentic give-and-take in these relationships. Each recognizes the importance of understanding and respecting the other's preferences, evaluations, and styles of caring.

"It's easy for caregivers to fall into the trap of feeling that they are doing everything right and that parents are doing everything wrong," reflects a provider who also is a workshop presenter. "I talk about this in the classes I teach, how caregivers blame parents and parents blame providers. I tell my [students] that it has to be a partnership."

"These [families] are going to be with me for a long time," explains another provider who lives in a small town in New York. "They respect the way I feel during the day and trust what I do. I have to trust what they do at night."

A California provider puts her emphasis on flexibility. "Parent-provider relationships make or break the business. [Parents] don't come into your home like a friend or a relative. They're clients. You have to bend and be flexible. You can't be cut-and-dried in your judgment."

Another reflects that "it is important to set limits [for yourself] by respecting parents as heads of their own households." A provider who conducts workshops for her child care resource and referral agency agrees: "You can't be didactic in family child care. The lines between parent and caregiver are too mushy."

Providers who work with children year after year see all kinds of families. Over the years, a hundred or more children might pass through their care. Many parents lack the confidence that experience has given providers. Quality caregivers have a deep understanding of parents—especially those who are beginners—like the one described in this provider's story:

"Erin's mother took her to the park on a wrist leash. Someone criticized her and she took it hard. I tell her she's doing a good job. Erin's a good kid and [her mom] is doing a good job of raising her. I can see mistakes she's making. They're probably the same ones I made, but sometimes you need to make mistakes [to] learn."

Respect doesn't come automatically, even for providers who have been in the business a long time. It's hard to let people blunder in the lives of children you love, even if they are the parents. Often it takes vigilance and a willingness to let go of control over the lives of people you care about. Providers have to remind themselves, and sometimes those around them, to approach each situation with acceptance and understanding.

"A child in my care was fed four doughnuts in the morning before she arrived at my house," reveals an experienced provider. "I thought, 'How could you do that!' I was the original Earth Mother and I made all my children's baby food, but I understand what [the parents] do. They feel a little guilt because they've left her all day long and so they sugar-love her.

"This child often has diarrhea on Mondays. My husband says, 'Why don't you yell at them?' But I really have to accept their values. It's their values and their child, I tell him."

Commitment to Conflict Resolution ~ Conflicts are a normal part of any human endeavor, even when people are working toward common goals. Nowhere is this more true than in family child care. All parents occasionally run late, forget to restock diaper bags, or try to manipulate policies. Providers sometimes surprise parents with unplanned time off, frustrations with children, and policy changes. It's normal to experience minor irritation now and then. Problems become serious when parents and caregivers let these irritations build and blame one another instead of working to resolve problems while they are still manageable.

Most of us are not accustomed to resolving conflicts with others. We feel we should be able to overlook irritations or work them out within ourselves; we're uncomfortable exposing our neediness or concerns to others. When we fail to handle things on our own, we become exasperated and lash out, or find fault. Successful parents and providers know that good relationships are strengthened by working through conflicts together. "I learned that I could be vulnerable and that mistakes could be laid at my feet," mused a reflective provider, "and parents could get angry and I could too, but no one had to walk out the door."

A thoughtful California provider knows how difficult the learning process can be. "Family child care providers don't have other staff to relieve them or an institutional structure to fall back on to help resolve problems. [When I first started] I was under the impression I could be all things to all people. I had to learn which types of families I could work with and which were beyond my limits."

"Sometimes my first encounter is antagonistic," says another. "These people often become the ones I am closest to in the end. We hash things out and get closer. 'No! I don't just baby-sit,' I tell them. Gradually relationships get onto a mutually respectful note."

A veteran Georgia provider puts it all together. "I always tell parents to tell me about anything that bothers them before it is a big problem. I may or may not be able to adjust things, given the needs of the group, but communication is the first step. Even then, conflict resolution isn't easy.

"One time, I had arranged a sleeping place for the baby on the enclosed side porch, so he could nap without being disturbed by the older children who were on a different rest cycle. It was late fall and I had begun thinking about where I would move him when it got cold, but I hadn't felt it was necessary to move him yet.

"One day, his mother arrived with a portable heater. She was too shy to open the conversation any other way, but she had been worried that he was getting cold at nap time. My first reaction was to feel hurt. Why couldn't she just tell me she was concerned? But she wasn't being judgmental. She just thought that her baby might be cold before I did. She didn't make a lot of fuss. She just came up with an easy way to solve the problem and meet everyone's needs, as I had recommended in our first interview. I was amazed, and I felt so supported, once I understood!"

More complicated conflicts require dedicated efforts, but they are worth the trouble. A veteran problem-solver shares this memory: "[My own] child was aggressive to a family day care child who was a passive victim. I wanted to say to the victimized child: 'Don't take it!' To sympathize with the aggressor, who was my own child, required a tightrope walk for a long time. The other mother and I both had to take time to support one another's child. And we had to support each other. We worked at knowing and liking each other. We said to the children that this relationship matters!"

Caregivers struggle not to play favorites when conflicts arise between children or with parents. The effort to nurture all children regardless of their behavior teaches providers to find common ground with parents. "When I don't like a child, for a period, I force myself to get closer, because usually if I do that, we can push through the uncomfortable time. I realized that this was something I needed to do with parents I felt uncomfortable with too. I needed to work on the friendship. Maybe that's why parents I had conflicts with have become my closest friends. I work very hard at getting to know them as people and appreciating who they are. I've come to treasure the friendships which come out of relationships where there's been a little conflict."

A provider who teaches conflict-resolution skills has a formula for working through problems with parents. "I go through a few simple steps to find solutions. Just knowing how to approach irritations helps keep everything manageable. First, I identify the problem. For example, 'Is it the disruption of a late pick-up that is bothering me, or the parents' unappreciative attitude when they arrive?' Next, I collect more information about the cause of the conflict and our mutual needs. I'll talk with the parents and try to find out why they arrive late so often. I ask them if they realize how their actions are affecting me and ask if they see an end to late pick-ups.

"Next, we brainstorm possible solutions, trying to find a way to make it win-win. Like, 'Should we double the late fee to make it worth my while? Should I ask them to do something helpful for me in return for flexibility? Should I give them three more chances to improve before terminating?' Then we pick a solution that seems to fix the root of the problem. For example, 'I am willing to be flexible and support their needs if they can do backup care for me when I have to leave early now and then.'

"Finally—and this is the most important part—we decide how to put the plan in place, how we will recognize success, and how long we will give it before we re-evaluate and try a new solution, if one is necessary. It takes a little time, but it really works to process conflicts this way!"

Support for the Family's Integrity ~ Quality caregivers value strong parent-child bonds. They know that children do not love their caregivers more than they do their parents, no matter how it seems at the moment. And they wouldn't want it any other way.

These providers do not come between the parent-child bond; they recognize that parents are the dominant force in their children's lives. They know that parents and caregivers who share in the care of young children have different but clearly complementary roles. The provider's relationship to a young child may be loving and tender; the two of them may feel an affection that is deep and long lasting. But the provider is not the child's parent, and collaborative providers don't try to be.

"I don't want parents or children to think of me as a replacement parent. I tell that to very young children when they're upset, and I tell parents the same thing. It's natural for children to choose

the parent over the caregiver. Children would like their parents to be at the caregiver's all day."

On this same theme, another provider reports: "One parent asked me if I would love her child. I said I would but never the way she does; no one will ever love her child the way she does; no one can take her place."

For many, the confusion is the strongest during the toddler years, when children are just learning to talk. Almost all providers have stories about toddlers who call them "Mommy." Long-term caregivers are sensitive to the pain this can cause. Although they know it is a common occurrence, it is difficult for some parents, especially mothers, because they worry that they have lost that special place in their children's hearts.

Some parents try to make light of the issue while hiding their hurt, but the misnaming feeds their feelings of loss and guilt. "It's hard enough for parents to go off to work without having the child call the caregiver 'Mommy,'" a California provider explains. She made sure this name was reserved for the child's real mother.

One mother says it became easier when she heard her one-year-old son say, "More, Mommy," to a four-year-old boy who was feeding him. "Suddenly, I saw that to him *Mommy* was a function, not a person. It was his all-purpose word for *Nurturer*. For a while, he even called his father Mommy, whenever Pete was feeding or rocking him."

Because this issue comes up again and again in child care, most providers develop ways of handling it and reassuring the parents. They let parents know the confusion is normal and does not reflect on their own parent-child connection.

"I kept telling them not to call me 'Mommy,' but new kids would come into the program, and it wasn't working," remembers a provider. "Now the kids call me Mommy Carol. The parents don't mind, and no one gets upset."

At Lynn's house, an assistant solved the problem by calling herself "Louie." The provider copied her and began to call herself "Lynnie." The name caught on with the kids because it seemed to fit in with "Mommy" and "Daddy." When a child calls either of them "Mommy," they act as though it is a joke and say, "I'm not Mommy, I'm Lynnie (or Louie)! Where's Mommy? Mommy is at work."

Family support also means supporting family decisions, even the confusing ones. "When I was going to graduate school, I offered care part-time," says a California provider. "One of the families hired a woman to care for their child when I wasn't available. The woman wanted the boy to be neat and clean. I always let him go outside and get dirty and moosh around. Even though we are different, I had to acknowledge what she does for the boy and give her credit for that. It's part of the circle of care giving. I think about the long-term wonderfulness of this—about what's going to be terrific and special because this child has [all these different caring people in his life]."

A provider who is trained as a counselor believes that care-givers support families by accepting their standards and priorities. For example, she sees no point in teaching the child of affluent parents to live the frugal way she does. "The right thing for the child is to be able to live with her parent. If the parent wants the child to go to a prestigious academic school, the kid will have to live with that. It doesn't make sense to support a different way for that child. I may have different views, but I wouldn't impose them. The child will have to negotiate with her own parent about high school and college and needs to be able to do that."

Sensitivity to Guilt and Loss ~ High-quality providers empathize with the way working parents feel when they leave their children each day. They sense their loss, their guilt, and their anxiety at entrusting a child to the care of another. They are able to stand in the parents' shoes and experience the challenges they face without judging them for the choices they have made.

"Before I had kids, I didn't understand parents," a California provider mused. "After I had to put my own child into day care, I

 appreciated what a parent goes through when she goes to work outside the home. [I had a child in care who] had a bad time with transition and separation. It's easier when a parent doesn't play into this, but this boy's parent couldn't leave when he was upset. She sometimes burst into tears when the child was crying. The mom was making it so much harder on the child....But this is a kid who never was cuddly—he was too excited by the world—and the mom was getting to hold him. So I said we'd just ride through it. The mom understood it might be a longer transition for the child, but she needed this time too. Moms have a hard time leaving very young children."

It is also painful for parents to miss their children's milestones—the first tooth, the first steps, the first word. Sensitive caregivers handle these events in different ways. Some don't refer to memorable moments, even if the tooth is poking through the gum, until the parents notice. Some tell the parent outright, so they can celebrate the accomplishment together. Either way, they are in sympathy with the parents' feelings.

"When a child takes a step or says a word, I tell parents what's happened," says one veteran caregiver. "But I can see why providers don't tell parents. I wish parents could be flies on a wall. I take photos so parents can see...."

Another thoughtful caregiver justifies a different approach: "If a child cuts a tooth or takes a first step, I don't tell the parent. I tell them it looks like he's just about ready to walk. I make sure the parent is paying attention. I want the parent to have the pleasure of seeing an accomplishment that most appropriately takes place at home. Being a parent is special, and I don't want to deprive parents of that enormous pleasure. I want to encourage their pleasure in their children as much as possible. I don't want them to feel threatened by me, or to feel that I am more the mother than they are."

"Humor helps," says a provider who tries to keep the situation light. "I joke from the beginning that it doesn't matter how many steps a child takes at my house; the 'first' step is the first one the parent sees. The same with first teeth and crawling. They don't count until the parents notice them and celebrate. When I suggest they pay attention because their child looks 'ready' to pop a tooth, we both know that the tooth may already be out, but everyone plays along. Most of my parents enjoy my little charade. We all know about reality, but it helps them take any 'non-firsts' I notice in stride."

Quality providers are also sensitive to parents' loss of personal time. Working parents quickly learn to sacrifice leisure time and socializing. When they aren't working, they wash clothes, cook, shop, clean, and run errands. Some providers try to help parents relax at the end of the day.

"I wanted parents to get to know each other," says a provider who is attuned to pressures on working parents. "They could have cheese and crackers or hang around for a half hour after my formal pick-up time. I wanted them to develop a sense of community with one another."

Family support is rarely a nine-to-five proposition. Some caregivers give parents time off on weekends and evenings by organizing overnights, camping trips, and visits to amusement parks. Some bend their rules on late fees and encourage parents to take personal time after work now and then. Dedicated providers know that parents need time to refresh themselves if they are to be truly present with their children. They make the extra effort because they know the value it has for the children.

Providers Are Professional ~ Family child care providers are not baby-sitters! "I haven't sat on a baby yet!" reads a popular T-shirt for sale at many family child care conferences. "When parents call and say they're looking for a baby-sitter," says one determined provider, "I tell them to talk to my teenage daughter. If it's a child care provider they want, they can talk to me."

Although family child care training supports business and education models for interaction, many new providers have a hard time being strict or businesslike with parents. Most caregivers learn through experience that they are professionals who run small, highly specialized, demanding, home-based businesses, and that every relationship with parents has to have a more formal side. Even well-loved parents must be viewed as clients who pay for services rendered in a timely, predictable manner. Experienced providers know that relationships differ from family to family, provider to provider, and situation to situation.

Professional providers learn to begin with good matches. They screen families at initial interviews before they agree to provide services. They compare philosophies of care, attitudes toward guidance and discipline, and expectations. They review the child's medical history, likes and dislikes, and family routines. If the child is very young, some talk about the bonds that will grow between them and the children. If the mother is working outside of the home for the first time, they talk about how the family feels about this change. Conscientious caregivers make a point of explaining state or local regulations and pointing out required equipment such as smoke detectors, fire extinguishers, and safety covers on outlets.

Another mark of professionalism is a signed contract between parents and provider. These written agreements spell out services provided, hours of operation, fees, and policies. Policies usually include information about unplanned absences, vacations, sick child care, emergencies, and daily schedules. Some agreements also include house rules on such things as behavior, expectations for trying new foods, and outlines of daily routines.

Veteran providers are nearly unanimous in the view that written contracts are critical to professional service. Written agreements clarify expectations and minimize conflict and confusion. "I take my contract seriously," says one provider who has been using contracts

for years. "I tell the parents there are a few things I won't be pushed on. Other things have some give."

Most use interview processes and contracts that have, according to one provider, "evolved over time to reflect areas of past misunderstanding. I do home visits now before enrolling children, and one thing I do besides a contract is to talk with parents about toddlers and the likelihood of biting or other kinds of aggression. I tell them that we don't know if their child is to be recipient or aggressor. A two year old's behavior can be very difficult, and I tell them that we'll need to work together. We can't get angry with other people's children....I train the parents before it happens, so it doesn't escalate. Parents have learned to approach this patiently and trust that I will help them take care of it.

"Another thing I discuss with parents ahead of time is playing outside. They [sometimes] play in puddles in winter, and this is a source of conflict. Parents think this is why children get colds. So at home visits I talk about these things too."

A male caregiver tries to spell out controversial policies in advance. "In my household, no weapons or war play is allowed. If I see them pretending to use something as a weapon, they will have to stop. I feel that way because [I don't like] the energy children feel when they play war—the negativism of somebody killing somebody. Parents have to understand that. [My views] sometime come out in the interview process. Or they come out when a child wants to bring a weapon. It's one of my rules, and I'm pretty firm about it."

Contracts and policy guidelines also spell out lines between business and friendship. Professional providers may draw these lines differently, but all draw them clearly. Using the business model, some providers avoid caring for children of friends or interacting socially with parents as part of their policies. They have found that it is harder to let go of a friend than a client when firmness becomes necessary.

"Now that I have spots open, I've taken in friends' kids, and it's really hard," says a provider who tries to be accommodating. "Sometimes you feel abused. You don't feel like saying, 'Because you and I are friends, you think you can overstep that rule.' So I like to keep a business line."

Others give friendship a clear place in the arrangement. One veteran of fifteen years says, "I tell parents that I might do them a favor now and then as a friend, but it's not part of my business. Keeping a child overnight is beyond my business arrangement, and I won't do it for pay. But I might help parents out as a friend when I know they need the favor. And as my friend, I expect them to do a favor like that for me too now and then and take my daughter overnight for me. When I put it this way, some parents never ask again, and that's just fine. Others are happy to keep the favors in balance and work to support my needs as I do theirs."

In addition to policy guidelines, many thoughtful professionals keep parents informed about their program design. When they make purchases—posters, or a puzzle, or a parakeet—they tell parents why. If they change the design of the environment—to set up a housekeeping corner or plant a garden—they explain how it meets the developmental needs of children. Some also share magazine articles and handouts from workshops that highlight and validate the work they do.

For the past two decades, increasing numbers of providers have demonstrated professionalism by joining or starting peer-support associations, by becoming credentialed, and by seeking out (or developing) specialized training. Most professional providers have wall displays or notebooks containing their proof of commitment to the profession. They might include their state or local regulatory certificate, membership in the National Association for Family Child Care (NAFCC), membership in their local association, a Child Development Associate (CDA) credential, NAFCC accreditation certificate, or other training certificates that say proudly, "This is my business, and I'm serious about it."

Parent-Provider Relationships and Quality Care

In its simplest terms, quality child care rests on the ability of a provider to develop a genuinely caring relationship with each child in the group. The well-known "indicators of quality" that have come out of current research—small group size, low adult-child ratios, and well-trained caregivers—are all elements in child care settings that promote caregiver-child relationships. Parent-caregiver relationships are not noted directly as quality indicators in these studies, but no one doubts their connection to excellent care.

A professional provider would never knowingly slight a child because of a weak relationship with parents, and yet interactions between adults do impact the more private connections, the life-long bonds, the quiet choices of the human heart. It is predictable that a caregiver would reach out and bond to the children of parents who welcome this connection. It's human nature.

Adult bonds enhance relationships between providers and children because they encircle the children with love. When parents and caregivers work closely together to raise children, respect and caring flows back and forth between them. Together, they venture beyond traditional limits into the deeper realms of collaboration, teamwork, friendship, and family.

Parents and providers who combine the family model with those of businesses and schools are exploring new frontiers in human relations, especially if they began the relationships as strangers. Under the direction of their own hearts, they are clearing pathways and building new roads of quality care for children. Their example invites us to join them in discovering its possibilities and its treasures.

Chapter 3

The outcome of any project always reveals, however subtly, the kind of energy that went into its development.

~ **J. D. Walters**

Special Circumstances

NAP TIME CIRCUS ❧ *TJ's mother called just before nap time. Keisha, the provider, wanted to talk. It was TJ's first day and she knew Marsha, his mother, was worried, but the call couldn't have come at a worse time.*

"He's doing fine," Keisha said, with her ear to the phone and an eye on the children. "At first, he just stood and watched the other kids play, but when the blocks came out, he joined right in. He ate a good lunch, macaroni and cheese and a lot of carrots! He must love carrots! I'm just settling them down for their naps now."

Or she had been. Four-year-old Jason was standing on his mat, twirling his blanket over his head like a lasso. Keisha cupped her hand over the phone. "Jason, please lie down! It's nap time. It's time to get calm and quiet."

Ignoring her, the boy strode purposefully into the kitchen. Keisha wasn't surprised. Jason had been diagnosed as hyperactive with attention deficit disorder, and he rarely followed instructions if they weren't enforced with immediate action. Now Keisha's attention was stretched three ways.

"I think TJ will do fine," she said again, reassuringly into the phone. "He seems tired. When the others quiet down, I think he will too. If he doesn't, I'll rock him or rub his back."

Somehow, Jason's blanket caught on a nail protruding from a beam on the ceiling. Keisha watched warily as he pushed a chair across the kitchen floor. He climbed up and began tugging on the blanket. Clearly, it was time to finish the phone call—and quickly!

"Why don't you call back in an hour to see how he's doing? I need to go and see about the children now."

She hung up the phone, hurried into the kitchen, and caught Jason just as the chair slipped out from under him. The boy was indignant. "It's your daddy's fault!" he said, accusing Keisha's carpenter husband. "He's the one who left that stupid nail up there!"

The craziness of Jason's allegation made Keisha smile. She wouldn't have thought of that in a lifetime. "Eli must have left it there to keep me on my toes," she said laughing. "He knows there's never a dull moment with four boys in day care." She picked up the chair and led Jason back to the other children.

"How would you like to hear a book about the circus?" she asked TJ and the others who had been watching from their mats. She pulled the book from a shelf, settled Jason safely onto her lap, and began to read.

Some Care Requires Special Skills

Rare is the group without at least one child who needs extra love and attention from grown-ups. Some children come from homes marked by stress, anger, abuse, or neglect. Others, by their nature, are overwhelmingly sensitive, shy, or clingy. Some live with diabetes or cerebral palsy; others have developmental delays, autism, or hyperactivity. The ability to cope with a range of needs is a necessity for most caregivers.

To nurture all the children enrolled in their programs, providers need skill, knowledge, versatility, and a high energy level. For youngsters like Jason, who are impulsive and relatively fearless, patience is required in large doses, and the ability to see the lighter side is a must. Safety is an important concern with children who are impulsive or quick to anger. Accurate information about diet is essential in caring for children with food allergies or diabetes.

Children who have some special needs are part of the normal spectrum of children in care. They have many of the same needs of any child. Providers must learn special skills and new information, without losing sight of typical patterns of development. Their businesses depend on it.

Working with Parents of Children with Disabilities ~ Relationships with parents of children with disabilities require extra thought and sensitivity. Many families experience some emotional turmoil when they realize that their children will not be able to accomplish things that other children seem to do without effort. They may go through a period of grief and longing as they struggle to accept the fact that

milestones other families take for granted—such as reading a book or pumping a swing—may be out of reach.

Experienced providers help families in whatever ways they can. Some parents require support for their own healing and patience as they adjust to their children's circumstances. Some need help answering disturbing questions: *Why us? How will we manage? Who will teach us what to do?* Those who become unraveled and distraught need compassion and understanding. Parents who blame one another for their children's disabilities and let grief take its toll on family life need sympathy and support.

With time, most families learn to be advocates for their children. High-quality caregivers join parents in seeking out workshops, books, and resource people who can provide needed services. They help to shoulder the load by listening. They accompany parents to meetings with specialists and open their homes to professionals who will work with the child. Providers also act as liaisons, introducing parents to other families who share or understand their situation.

Coping with Denial ~ Providers working with parents who have accepted the fact that their child is not developing typically are fortunate because they can act as a team from the beginning. Many caregivers, however, are not this lucky; especially when they are the first to observe that a child does not appear to follow normal developmental patterns. When this happens, the challenge is twofold. The provider must work constructively with the child and help educate the parents who may be unaware or in denial. Months can pass before everyone agrees that there might be a problem. This double duty takes a toll.

A veteran urban provider cared for a four year old who was unable to name simple everyday objects such as scissors, raincoat, car, and cat. When the child tried to communicate, her sentences were often garbled and unintelligible. Although the provider was fairly certain the parents needed to take the child to be evaluated by a professional, she did not think the family was likely to do so because they spoke "baby talk" to the girl. Nevertheless, the caregiver gathered her courage, shared her observations and concerns with the parents, and recommended that they take the child to be tested. As predicted, the parents refused. The child was "still a baby" they insisted; she would speak more clearly when she was older.

The provider respected the parents' right to make decisions for the child, but she became increasingly uncomfortable with their attitude as the weeks passed and evidence of language delay grew stronger. She felt torn between her wish to do what was right for the child and her responsibility to support the family.

Providers who find themselves in situations like this often become frustrated. It can seem that there is no way around the impasse. Those who have information about child development and access to community resources do better, especially if they are able to empathize with the parents.

The caregiver in this situation was able to get the help that was needed. She voiced her concerns to a visiting child care specialist. The specialist agreed with the caregiver's assessment, and on the strength of this, the provider approached the parents again. This time they consented to testing. With the help of a speech therapist, the family and the provider were able to work together as a team.

Contending with Abuse and Neglect ~ Many circumstances prevent families from giving children the care they need. Some parents are too preoccupied with responsibilities, careers, or personal advancement to pay adequate attention to a child's development. Some fail to notice a child because they have to work two jobs to pay their bills. Some are overwhelmed by a personal crisis, while others lack adequate information on child development.

In some communities, children who are neglected or mistreated at home are placed in family child care during the day, for their own protection. Providers who care for these children are often unhappy witnesses to the effects of abuse or neglect. Children may come in the morning wearing the same dirty clothes they wore the day before. Others arrive clean but overtired, angry, frightened, sad, or withdrawn. A few beg to be allowed to stay with the provider at the end of the day.

As mandated reporters of child abuse, caregivers are required by law to notify authorities if they think a child is in danger, but many situations are not clear-cut. Many situations may be painful but not serious enough to report to professional services.

Providers must find constructive ways to love and bond with these children and to their families, despite what may happen on weekends or at night. Skilled caregivers begin with the understanding that, most importantly, children need the love and care of their own families. They make a point of supporting stressed-out parents by listening to them at the end of the day. They know that fifteen minutes of supportive listening may give parents the emotional space they need to offer the same understanding and support to their children later that evening.

But providers must be aware of their own limitations; pressures on families may be overwhelming and parents may not be able to give their children consistent love and care. When this is the case, caregivers must provide children with an oasis of caring during the day and be ready to let go of them at night. This delicate balance can be painful and difficult to achieve, especially when caregiver-child bonds run deep. But it goes with the job; each family's challenges must be accepted and understood.

Balancing the Needs of the Individual with Those of the Group ~

Most providers become adept at juggling varying needs and abilities—the three year old who is withdrawn and shy, the toddler who is asthmatic, the school-aged child who is impulsive, the four-year-old chatterbox who continually asks why. They see this as part of their job description and look beyond specific needs to the heart of the child. They build on their interests, share their discoveries, laugh at their jokes, and rejoice in their accomplishments. Skilled providers take differences in stride.

Not all parents are comfortable with these arrangements, however. They are ashamed or unhappy when their children have bad days or are difficult to manage and feel guilty asking for help or

special consideration. By the same token, parents of children who tend to be less demanding can find it difficult to accept the fact that other children require more attention, especially when problems are behavioral or emotional. They want to be sure that their own children get enough nurturing too.

Parental comfort concerning the balance of the group is left to the skill and intuition of the provider. Because of the small numbers and wide range of variables, no two child care groups are ever alike. High-quality providers reassure parents that their children are happy and busy most of the day. They see to it that each child is relaxed in the caregiver's presence and that each one knows the warmth of her love. In order for the children to thrive, parents must feel they have made the right child care decision, and each provider must have the peace of mind to keep it all together—at least most of the time.

How Do High-Quality Providers Manage?

>*❧* **FAMILY CHILD CARE** is frequently the setting of choice for families in special circumstances. The small setting and the willingness of home-based providers to adjust their hours, rates, and policies to give families individualized help makes it ideal.

Given the demands and the responsibilities, how do providers manage? Why do they agree to offer care to a child like Jason? How do they balance the needs of the individual with the needs of the larger group? How is it possible for them to bend over backward to help troubled families without losing their balance? What do these parent-provider relationships look like? Most providers have learned to answer these questions through experience.

Set Clear Limits ~ In affluent suburbs, low-income urban neighborhoods, and small rural towns, family child care providers care for children with challenging behaviors. Many make a career out of it! Some of their charges are diagnosed as hyperactive or emotionally disturbed, but the majority are "simply" strong-willed, impulsive, independent, active children who haven't learned to follow directions or control their own impulses.

How do they behave? An older preschooler may not be able to finish a puzzle, complete a building blocks project, draw a picture, or put away toys without close supervision. They may be impulsive and lack a sense of personal danger. They climb too high, run too fast, jump when they should be standing, bounce when they should be sitting. They may take risks that endanger children who happen to be nearby. If they're on a riding toy, they pedal so fast they threaten the nearest toddler. If they're dancing to music, they move so vigorously that they bump into the other children.

Children who are considered challenging generally have poor social skills and have trouble making or keeping friends. They may hit other children for no apparent reason and cry noisily when they are angry or frustrated, but when they are the cause of the problem, they don't even notice. Calmer children their own age generally avoid them; older children frequently resent their noisy disruptiveness.

Most providers understand that a complex array of factors contributes to a child's difficulties, and they know the importance of setting clear limits. Their rules are simple and well defined. "We talk about what they can do and what they can't," explains one caregiver. "I tell them they have to keep their hands 'to home.' They can't hit, or push, or touch children who don't want to be touched. They have to use quiet 'indoor voices.' They have to treat the house and one another with respect."

Caregivers hold to these guidelines even when children or families complain. "Some children tell me I'm not fair because they don't have to follow rules at home," says another provider who also believes in setting limits. "But I just tell them that we have different rules at my house. Most understand that and we don't have any problems."

Providers aren't surprised when parents ask questions about how to keep children focused and "under control." Many feel parents are afraid to say no, even if the rule is for the child's own good. "I tell these parents if you want your child to listen, you have to tell him so he'll listen," says another firm provider. "If you're crossing the street, you tell him to hold your hand and you don't take no for an answer. It's the same thing in the house. You're the adult. He'll listen, if you tell him. You just have to say no!"

Although rules are fast and firm, high-quality providers are soft when it comes to love. They hug and kiss the children when they are cooperative, hold them when they're sad, and rock them when they're tired. "A lot of these children don't get enough affection at home. They need to be where they're safe and loved," says an urban caregiver who doesn't demand that unhappy children "pull themselves together"—even for official-looking visitors. She cuddles out-of-control children on her lap until they are ready to be back on their own.

Do challenging children ever learn to accept boundaries? It depends on the child, but clear rules enable most to begin learning the basics for interacting with others. They learn to ask other children for toys rather than to take them, and they learn to express themselves with words, rather than with their hands and feet, when they are frustrated. Those who are guided with firmness and kindness in their early years often start school with good self-esteem and are better able to cope with that more impersonal system.

Communicate in Writing ~ Every book on relationships talks about the importance of communication, and child care relationships are no exception. Successful providers and parents talk freely and openly about the children's activities, events that impact the children's lives, and the family's expectations for her care. When children and circumstances at home are peaceful, it is possible for these exchanges to take place casually in the morning, at the end of the day, or during an occasional evening phone call. When children have extraordinary needs, however, communication has to be more regular and more thorough.

A provider with a master's degree in special education says she asks the parents of children diagnosed with attention deficit hyperactivity disorder (ADHD) to use a daily journal to record their concerns. "Children who are [diagnosed with] ADHD have to learn to internalize adult rules and expectations," she says. "It is very important for all adults to have consistent routines and expectations. A quick exchange at the door in the morning when the parent is anxious to leave for work isn't enough; neither does it make sense to try to talk at the end of the day when the child is eager to go home."

She tells the story of Chad's parents who understood the importance of consistent supervision. They didn't look forward to writing every day, but they knew its value. Their son had been in a preschool program in which problems were analyzed in writing, and they had seen its benefits. They used the notebook to describe the child's behavior at home and to ask questions and make suggestions.

"Chad fell asleep today at the dinner table. We'd like him to be able to stay awake longer, if it's possible. Do you think he would nap at your house if you put him down later? Would it disturb your schedule? On the weekends, he naps in the afternoon as late as 2:00 or 3:00."

The provider used the journal as a way to describe the child's behavior in child care and her response. "Yesterday, while Chad was playing Legos, another parent dropped off a child. Chad stopped playing and did everything he could think of to get my attention. He threw balls in the air, climbed on the kitchen counter, and interrupted me when I talked with one of the parents. Today, I wanted him to be more controlled when this parent came. Just before she was to arrive, I took him aside and explained that I wanted him to continue playing while the parent was here. I asked him to save his questions until she left. When she came to the door, I reminded him again. Chad did very well. He stayed in the living room and quietly built a spaceship. He didn't interrupt and didn't run around. After the parent left, I thanked him and hugged him and told him he did a good job. I gave him a sticker for his sticker book, and he was pleased and proud."

This written dialogue, although time-consuming, gradually strengthened the family's management practices. The boy's mother and father believed that consistency was important, but the two of them managed their son quite differently. The father expected Chad to respond quickly to his instructions, while the mother relied more on reward and indirection. Their provider's comments gave the family new ideas and strengthened strategies that worked.

Written communication enables love to flow where it is most needed. When Chad's parents put their thanks into writing, they strengthened the provider's resolve to give to the child, no matter what happened during the day. When they apologized for a tiring weekend and he was disruptive on a Monday morning, they gave the caregiver deeper reserves of patience and understanding. Written communication helped the parents too. The love and commitment that were revealed in the provider's painstaking descriptions inspired and fortified the parents when they were confused or overwhelmed at home.

With the help of the journal, these adults gradually grew into an effective team. The results were observable to friends and family members alike. Chad learned, without being asked, to take an adult's hand in a busy parking lot, to keep his seat belt buckled in the car, and to use verbal communication more often. His self-esteem and his relationships with the other children improved as well. He learned to play more cooperatively with children his own age and was able to apologize when he was in the wrong.

While the benefits of written communication are clear in this situation, less tangible benefits of a journal are equally important. When providers are lost in day-to-day details, the journal reminds them of the larger picture, enabling them to trace a child's progress and their own. When they're burned out, the act of writing helps to restore their objectivity. Journals become treasures beyond price as older children read about their infant selves through their providers' eyes. Nothing can take the place of long ago words documenting love shared, struggles surmounted, and joy experienced day by day.

Explain Program Goals ~ In high-quality programs, the needs of one child do not overshadow those of the others in care. Each family feels confident that the provider has enough love and energy to go around. One of the ways caregivers maintain this balance is by helping parents understand their program goals. Families who are able to see the group as a whole find ways to help one another; everyone works together for the same objectives.

For example, one experienced provider who accepted a child who was deaf into her program talked ahead of time with the parents of children who were already enrolled. "They all thought it would be a good experience for their kids to meet him and interact with him and learn that [people are] different in one way or another. Some can't hear, some can't walk, some can't talk....I told them I would be using sign language, and they were willing to have their children learn a little sign along the way."

In the beginning, the boy was frustrated because he didn't have the ability to communicate what he was feeling. "[At home] when he was put in time-out or sent to his room, he became destructive," explained the provider. "I helped him express himself by teaching him extra signs, particularly those that described variations in feeling. At the same time, I helped the other children and their parents understand the problem. 'Hearing people can just blurt their feelings out,' I told them. 'But he has to stop and think about how to express his feelings in sign language.'"

From time to time, the other families were critical of his interpersonal behavior and social skills. This provider helped them to understand that children who are deaf need to see when people use social amenities such as *please* and *thank you* because they can't hear them. They miss shades of feeling that are expressed through inflections and tone of voice. Someone needs to take time to explain what is going on and what is expected.

"I clarified for them why he became impatient when I was on the phone or talking to other children," she continued. "I helped them understand that he kept on tickling their children when they wanted him to stop because he couldn't understand what they were feeling. He couldn't count on facial cues to guide his behavior."

Thanks to this provider's patient explanations, the parents were able to see that the boy was basically a bright, active, lovable child. They passed on the image to their children and encouraged them to be understanding when the boy was frustrated and in need of help. Everyone helped the group stay in balance, and all were enriched.

When each family invests in a provider's vision, fears that one child is overtaxing the system diminish. Parents see that the experience is good for their children's moral development; they relax and trust that the others understand. In high-quality family child care homes, families and providers work together as a team for the good of each person in the group.

Use Parents as Resources ~ Providers are ultimately responsible for defining their own program goals, but parents often support them with insight and information. The parents of a child with asthma helped her provider and the group learn about that condition by obtaining written information on triggers from the American Lung Association. The parents of a child with attention deficit disorder paid the registration fee for an all-day conference on ADHD for themselves and their provider because they wanted to be sure they all had the latest information. The father of a child with Down's syndrome presented his son's provider with all the data he could find on that topic on the Internet.

Caregivers appreciate whatever information parents can supply about their children's conditions. Providers may have general knowledge, but parents know how to read their own children's needs. They can tell the difference between minor recurring problems and medical emergencies and know what comforts work best when their children are in distress.

A caregiver who had no direct experience with autism agreed to "go out on a limb" and care for Trent, a mildly autistic four year old, because the mother "seemed to know so much" when they talked at the interview.

"The mother knew I was inexperienced, but I told her I was willing to learn. She asked if it would be all right to have therapists come into my home to work with the child, and I said I didn't mind.

This made a big difference to her and to me too. She had been looking for a provider who would let people come in, and I liked the idea of having professionals around who could answer questions if I ran into problems.

"The mom and I talked several times before Trent actually started coming to my home. She told me about his diet and some of his sensitivities. He can become distracted by noises that people usually don't hear, like electrical humming, and he is very picky about food. She told me about his repetitive behaviors too. He spins plates, and he likes to put his toys into neat straight lines.

"She also explained about the therapy. She told me the therapists' schedules and talked about their methods. She offered to lend me books, if I wanted to read about their approach.

"The first couple of weeks I was nervous, but I liked Trent right off and the feeling just grew stronger. In a lot of ways he's like any child. He flaps his arms sometimes when he's excited, and he gets upset when the children don't sit 'in the right chairs,' but he likes to play with the blocks, and he loves it when the other children join in."

She stopped to think for a few minutes. "I'm not saying I haven't had problems. One time, Trent got so upset he started biting his own arm. I'd never seen a child do anything like that— usually they hurt other people—and I didn't know what to do. I was pretty upset and the children were too. I hated to do it, but I called the mom at work. She was okay. She explained that he was probably angry or frustrated and told me what I could do to comfort him. I did what she said, but it took a long time for him to calm down.

"That night after the children were in bed, we talked for a while on the phone. She said that it isn't uncommon for children like Trent to hurt themselves when they're upset. I apologized for calling, but she said I did the right thing. That helped a lot.

"I've had Trent for two years now. He's in school and he's doing pretty well. He's potty trained, and he can speak in complete sentences if he wants to."

Reflecting on her experience, the provider concluded, "I'm glad I took him in. I've learned a lot about autism, I can tell you that! The family made all the difference. Especially the mom. She was so patient and she was so good at explaining things.

"I think I'd care for other children with special needs, if they came my way. It doesn't seem as hard as it used to. If the family can do it, I guess I can too."

Mentor Parents ~ It may seem natural for caregivers to partner with parents who are well informed, but they also need to know how to join forces with parents who lack parenting skills. Many adults with children in care have unrealistic expectations regarding their children's development. They aren't certain how to nurture children, offer guidance, or take care of their physical needs. Many have a limited capacity for empathy as well. They can't feel an infant's longing to be held, or a two year old's curiosity, or a preschooler's need for independence. Providers who care for the children of these parents routinely find themselves answering questions on topics from toilet training and diaper rash to runny noses and bedtime strategies.

When should my child begin to use the potty? What should I do if he has an accident? How can I get her to sleep at night? When should a two year old go to bed? How do I keep my child from helping himself to food in the refrigerator? How can I teach my child manners?

Mentoring is a natural role for experienced providers. They have spent years working with children from a variety of circumstances and backgrounds and know how to tell serious problems from normal developmental stages. Much of the time, they know when children need outside help and when they will outgrow troublesome behavior on their own. When parents don't have clear answers, they know how to find help.

Mentoring relationships go beyond sharing information about children and their care. As trust builds, parents and caregivers enter one another's lives. Relationships become more subtle, deeper, and more intricate. A rural provider in the Northeast remembers her deepening relationship with a mother she mentored who was "rigid, protective, and a meticulous housekeeper." The mother's rigidness had a profound effect on the whole family.

"The children weren't allowed to do the things normal kids do," explains the provider. "They couldn't go outside or to the park or the library. The parents didn't want the kids interacting with other kids.

"I watched these children for two years. Every day, in my house, we did something together. Simple things like sticking flowers on paper plates. Nobody had ever done things like that with those kids before.

"The mom watched the children and saw changes. I didn't tell her to do it 'my way.' You can't pounce on somebody and tell them that. These were her children, and I never wanted to take that away from her. But they were in my house and there was a blending.

"I took the kids to the library and took out books. They'd never gone to a library before in their lives. They got so interested in it! But the father didn't like my taking his kids everywhere. He thought babysitters should just keep kids inside and make sure they were safe.

"We convinced the mother, and one day those kids dragged their father to the library. We held our breath, but you could see the dancing in their eyes. He melted. The next thing I knew, they got library cards.

"[The mother] was flexible enough to discuss problems. At one point, she thanked me for being there. She told me she never had a mother or a sister to talk to....

"I couldn't believe it, but I touched the mother's life, changed her way of parenting....The family just needed to learn....They were never exposed. I think that's partly the role of day care. We go beyond child care and teach some of the parents too."

A veteran provider in a similar situation took on a toddler who was unpredictably aggressive, excessively angry, and frequently unwilling to make eye contact. He presented a huge challenge as a member of her child care group. But rather than give in to the urge to either take over or terminate the family, this provider chose to work with the mother as well as the child.

"MaryJean dearly loved her son, but something was off," recalls the caregiver. "He resisted being held, even as an infant; no one seemed to know why. One day, out of the blue, the boy's grandma came to town and spent a day with us. We had some talks that revealed that she and MaryJean had not developed strong attachments when MaryJean was a child. An older sibling had died right after she was born, and she was shuffled around from person to person for almost a year while her mother coped with her grief.

"The problem was being passed to the next generation. I knew I wouldn't be doing anyone any favors if I just got him to connect to me, so I started showing MaryJean how I deal with tantrums. I

encouraged her to hold him gently but firmly until he rebalanced, instead of freezing or walking out of the room. [I explained that] leaving a child like him alone, as punishment, feels like abandonment and makes everything worse.

"At first, the dad thought we were crazy, and he would try to rescue his son so he could 'scream it out.' He thought keeping him 'trapped' was abusive. So I wrote down exactly what I did and why. I explained how I loosen my hold as he gains self-control, how I use words to describe his feelings while he's venting, and how I wait until he relaxes and makes willing eye contact before letting him go. I showed both parents a book that validated my ideas and coached MaryJean when she tried the technique at my house.

"When the father began to see the results—gentle, caring behaviors toward the others, shorter tantrums, more focused attention span—he was convinced and began to try the technique himself. Now the child asks to be held! It's like a miracle to all of us. The whole family benefited from this mentoring. And I gained the delightful, normally mischievous two year old who I knew was in there all along!"

Mentoring parents who lack parenting skills isn't usually in a provider's job description; most get into the business because they love working with children, not adults. They take on this responsibility because they care deeply for the children and know the relationship is important for the children's happiness and well-being. Their commitment enables many children who are at risk to be safe, loved, and well cared for while their parents grow into the job.

Team Up with Teen Moms ~ Experienced providers often touch families' lives in deep, meaningful, and unexpected ways. They teach first-time parents about children's developmental needs and help them respond to out-of-bounds behavior calmly, creatively, and responsibly. Nowhere are these interactions more important than in the relationships between caregivers and teen moms.

"Teen moms are like any teenager," one provider clarifies. "They have the attitude—as we did—that they're going out to conquer the world. But they have this little person they're responsible for. It's hard because they've never had a life of their own.

"After the newness wears off, the baby isn't fun-and-games anymore. The baby gets up. The baby is sick. The baby cries and gets into things. The mom can't go out on a date because of the baby. Day-to-day problems have to be worked out."

Providers and teens sometimes develop relationships that are a cross between mother-daughter relationships and adult friendships. The advantage over the biological mother-daughter tie is that it is easier for each person to see the other's point of view. For teen moms who are uncomfortable asking for help or advice from their own mothers, a caregiver who cares can be critical. "I was looking for someone who could teach me. I knew I had a lot to learn. My mom was always telling me that, but I couldn't learn from her. I felt like she was always telling me what I did wrong. I didn't mind listening to my baby's caregiver. She just told me what I needed to know."

While the willingness to become involved is strong, the role of mentor can be confusing for the provider. "At first I wondered whether it was my job to take care of her or the child. But I know now. It's both."

A provider and a teen mom developed a close relationship that lasted several years. "I taught her a lot of little things she didn't know. I taught her to dress her son in socks and a hat in the winter when it was cold. I bought him a few pairs of socks and told her where she could buy others inexpensively. I taught her how to fold cloth diapers and showed her how to use cornstarch instead of those expensive ointments.

"When her son was two, he started biting. She disciplined him by washing his mouth out with soap and biting him back. I told her I couldn't discipline that way and talked about time-out. I told her to tell him the other child was hurt and show him the red marks on the other child's skin, without using violence.

"When the baby was two, the mom got pregnant again. She didn't have a car and I didn't want her to feel tied down, so I took her places on the bus. We talked about how she'd manage the children when they went out together. We went to the mall and the library and a few other places on a 'trial run.' I wanted her to be able to do things with her kids that they would enjoy, and so would her friends.

"My whole family cared about her. We wanted her to succeed. My father-in-law played with the children and drove them all home when the weather was bad. We were proud of the things she had learned to do with the children."

When the relationship is strong, teen moms develop confidence in their own abilities as parents. "I was always afraid someone would think I was a bad mom and take my child away. My baby's provider would tell me I wasn't a bad mother. She'd say, 'This is just something you are going through.'"

Bonds between teen moms and their babies' caregivers can run deep. Some teens drop in to visit after the caregiving period is over so the provider sees how much the baby has grown. Some call and send photographs. Some become friends and stay in touch for years.

Tap Outside Resources ~ Family child care providers do not always have the skills they need to work with children and their families. They don't always know how to bridge differences or explain their concerns in ways that parents can accept or understand. Deep-seated conflicts can occur over discipline, rules, and child-rearing philosophies. Differences can go undiscovered for months and flare up only after loving bonds are set. High-quality providers recognize their own limitations and look for resources to teach them the skills they need, rather than terminate a child who poses a challenge. Many attend workshops and join professional associations that give them opportunities for discussion with peers. Networking of this type is increasingly common.

Experienced providers also team up with specialists to ensure that care is at a high level. Although a long-term relationship with a professional consultant is unusual, most serious providers find ways to get support and assistance when they need it. The Family and Work Institute's 1994 *Study of Children in Family Child Care and Relative Care* found that providers who network with other professionals are more likely to provide high-quality care. Similarly, caregivers who support one another by problem-solving together are more likely to be responsive to children and families.

"I have a hard time with some of the families of children I care for," reports a professional provider who sought out such support. "When one of the children gets a bloody nose at home, the parents call me and ask me what happened in child care. [When they do that] I get defensive. Other times, the child will act out and be aggressive in my home, and I'll ask the parents whether anyone in the family is sick. [When I do that] I make them defensive.

"I called the consultant [at the hospital's infant-parent program] because I was concerned about a child who was very aggressive. I was trying to hire a new assistant, and this child was scaring away the applicants. I thought he needed help, but his parents couldn't see what was going on. He was their only child and they didn't see him with other kids very much. I asked the consultant to observe the child and tell me whether my concerns were really true."

The consultant confirmed that the child needed help, and she and the provider arranged to talk together with the parents. "The conference went well. The family was at ease because the consultant was there too. I was standing on the sidelines. The consultant asked a lot of questions about their family life and changes they'd gone through." With the consultant's help, the family and the provider were able to determine a course of action that would benefit the family and the child.

The provider gained a great deal from this relationship with an outside professional. "I learned a lot from seeing how [the consultant] handled conflict situations. I have had to learn to think before I respond. I've had to learn to say 'I'll get back to you on this,' rather than make a quick response. It takes a lot of self-reflection and work, but it's getting easier."

Accept Extra Risks ~ One of the biggest challenges a provider can take on is a child with life-threatening disabilities. Infants with cystic fibrosis need to have their lungs freed of fluid each day; children with asthma need to be put on inhalators; babies at risk for SIDS need to be monitored every time they go to sleep.

Providers' commitments to children with serious physical disabilities carry more than the usual amount of worry and uncertainty, especially if provider-child bonds are deep. Even if they know how to cope, the fears remain. *How will I feel if Tenesha has to be hospitalized? What will I do if Chris can't breathe, even on the inhalator? What if Lisa stops breathing while she is asleep?*

A surprising number of providers do take on these responsibilities, even when they are not trained as nurses or paramedics. They are aware of the uncertainties, but their concern for a child's well-being and ties to the child's family outweigh their fears.

A provider in a rural area found herself in this situation when a preschooler in her care was discovered to be diabetic. "We found out in October. The kids were playing and he was sleeping on the couch. The kids were pretty noisy but he didn't wake up. He was in diabetic shock. His mom had told me he might be diabetic; the doctor was doing some testing. She had given me glucose and told me what happened when a child goes into shock.

"I called my support to help watch the other children and called his mom. I tried to wake him. I gave him glucose, a little at a time, and gradually he came out of it.

"After that, his other child care provider—he had two—would send me a note to let me know his sugar level that particular day. I sent her a note back so she would know too. The notes were kept together so the mom would know what was going on for the whole day."

When the emergency was over, the provider asked her insurance agent whether she would be covered if the child convulsed or died. "He told me I wasn't. If the child died, I'd be on my own. I had to make a decision whether I wanted to continue with him or not. The insurance agent said a good business maneuver would be to let the child go, but I just didn't see the sense in it."

This provider's connection to the family and her love for the child led her to make what others might consider to be a poor business decision, but she is not alone in her willingness to go beyond personal liability to work with a family with critical needs. Why do providers do it? What's the payoff? Hard as it may be to believe in this day and age, the payoff for providers is love.

Love Is the Glue That Keeps Everyone Together

IN A WORLD WHERE CHILDREN are labeled as damaged and bounced from one setting to another in frightening numbers, it is wonderful to find evidence of loving alternatives. Love is the secret ingredient that gives caregivers the strength to work with challenging children when everyone is tired and stretched thin. It encourages providers to master specialized medical information, treatments, and care procedures. It allows their homes to be safe and caring sanctuaries for children who come to them from homes marked by violence and neglect. Love is what keeps caregivers on the job when more objective criteria suggests that they should pull back.

Love shared by providers is the invisible force that helps children thrive despite their circumstances. Love gives them the strength to persevere when their bodies are weak and their spirits are low. It gives the child who is hearing impaired the peace that is needed to learn sign language. It enables the child who is hyperactive to learn to follow directions. Love makes it possible for the child with asthma to accept the machinery needed to live with that condition.

The love that is found in high-quality family child care homes is not limited to children with disabilities or to those in special circumstances, nor is it limited to even the very young. It is the hidden element that touches every heart in care. Love for the children inspires providers to reach out to their parents as well. Motivated by providers who care, many parents return the feeling and love flows round and round, until everyone—no matter what the need—is encircled in love, making survival a shadow from the past.

Chapter 4

The Gate of Heaven

> *Life comes unexpectedly*
> *And the Gate of Heaven is everywhere,*
> *And so we tell ourselves to be*
> *Very careful*
> *And to proceed with caution—*
> *Or we may commit*
> *Love!*
>
> **~ David Pavlovich**

Redesigning the Family Circle

LOVE IS A ROSE ⟶ *Beth let the phone ring while she considered whether her child care children were engaged enough in their play to permit a short phone conversation. She hoped that the person on the other end of the line was a friend. She was feeling lonely and sorry for herself. It was spring break for the school-aged children, but instead of getting a break of her own, she was busier than usual, weaving older kids into her routine.*

"Maybe I should go back to teaching," she whined to herself for the fifth time that day. She reached for the receiver.

"Hello?"

"Hi! This is Rosie, Tommy's mom. It's spring break and I couldn't let any more time go by without calling you. You know, we had such a good time with you during the holidays, and I still miss talking to you every day, even though it's been years! I'm just wondering how you are."

"Oh! Hi, Rosie! I'm fine. Actually, all the school kids are here and I was wishing I was on spring break too. I was feeling jealous of teachers like you who have this time off. Are you and Tom having a good vacation? I thought of you last week. Did he enjoy his birthday?"

"Oh, yes, of course, and he appreciated your card! In fact, Tommy has something to tell you. He made me promise I wouldn't say it first, so maybe I'd better let him talk before I blurt it out. He's right here, breathing down my neck!"

Beth glanced back at her little ones who were chasing each other on the riding toys while the good-natured school-agers directed traffic along the "road" they had built with boards and pillows. She was delighted to have this unexpected opportunity to reconnect with one of her long-ago toddlers, who was now sixteen.

"Hello? Beth?"

"Hi, Tom, how are you?"

"I'm great! Thanks for the card last week. Guess what! I got my learner's permit yesterday! I'm learning to drive!"

"Oh, Tom! That's great! Maybe you can drive over here sometime and take me for a ride!"

Beth's heart filled with pride as she thought back to the time when Tom had driven these same toy cars, and then moved on to be the "police" in her family child care home. Her eyes teared a bit, missing that baby boy and realizing that it was important for him to share this big news with her. They chatted a little more, longer than most adults manage with young men at this awkward age. They discussed school and girls and his new experiments with cooking.

"Okay, guy, it's my turn again," broke in Rosie.

"Yeah, Mom, I'm done. I'm going over to Ray's house now, okay?"

"Sure, honey. Bye. Huh? No you can't take the car! Ha! Ha! So, Beth, do you have a few more minutes?"

Their conversation flowed as it had during child care years. They caught up on each other's lives, shared stories about their divorces, asked about each other's families, and added another layer of caring onto the friendship they had begun almost sixteen years ago. As Beth hung up she looked around at the photos in her living room. Tom's was there, and his buddy Nathan's, and Alaina's too. All three were children she had cared for who had grown up and kept in touch. On the chrome bookcase in the corner stood the photo Marie had sent of herself and Teddy. Marie *was the first child she had cared for to have a baby of her own. So many photos! So many families! So many good friends! "How many teachers would get a call like that?" Beth wondered, remembering once again why she loved her job.*

Revisiting Cultural Norms

The idea that a deep caring relationship between parents and providers could be one of the elements of quality care makes some people uncomfortable. "You're going too far!" cried a parent, in hot response to the suggestion that she should venture beyond traditional norms with her child's caregiver. "I have to have a life too!" protested an equally threatened caregiver during a relationship workshop.

There are many good reasons for holding to the current standard for parent-caregiver interactions. Our world is a busy place and each of us has limited amounts of time and energy. Many adults have close families or support groups and can't fit in any more relationships. Not all adults are inclined to make tight connections with the people they pay to perform a business service. Traditions and taboos regarding business-based friendships provide us with a level

of comfort and protection. Many parents and caregivers share respectful yet reserved relationships, and their children receive quality care, according to traditional guidelines and expectations.

So if it ain't broke, why try to fix it? The fact is, although our children are surviving, it's time to fix our awareness of what they really need to thrive. When parents and caregivers become close, something significant happens that enhances the quality of life for children and their families—

something too important to be discounted or overlooked. These friendships enrich children's lives long after the caregiving years, often impacting the next generation. Norms established by schools and businesses may not be broken, but something else works better for children in child care.

Adult and Child Needs Differ ~ With adults, relationships vary in depth and warmth, intimacy, and intensity. We have the ability to keep some people at a distance and interact casually with others, while nurturing and investing deeply in those we hold dear. Most adults have no problem—in fact, we are quite comfortable—with interactions that are matter-of-fact or businesslike. Acquaintanceships aren't negative or detrimental; we know from experience that, sometimes, well-constructed fences make good neighbors.

Current experts on adult communication styles point out that we like to keep our distance to preserve our uniqueness and independence. We need other people to survive, but we want to survive as individuals. At the same time, we feel an equally important impulse to get close to others, to develop community, to feel that we are not alone in the world.

This twofold movement accurately describes adult needs and interactions; however, the needs of children are different. Children need to feel attached, caught up in an unending web of love, bonded in a way that borders on engulfment, before they can benefit from distance and independence. They can't turn off their inclinations to give and receive love the way adults do. They need to feel surrounded by love, and free to return it. The younger the child, the more critical it is for all adults in that child's life to encircle her with love.

Selma Fraiberg, expert on child development and author of *The Magic Years* and *Every Child's Birthright*, calls attention to the importance of bonded attachments for very young children. She points to a critical need for stable, continuous, predictable human partnerships if children are to realize their fullest potential for love, trust, learning, and self-worth. Seamless, engulfing love is instinctive in children and indispensable for their development into independent, yet securely attached adults.

Immersion in love is important for children's cognitive development as well. The authors of *Heart Start: The Emotional Foundations of School Readiness* claim that there is a connection between the depth and nature of children's early attachments and their ability to learn. Confidence, responsibility, and trust in others develop when very young children have secure loving connections to adults. In the first months of life, children try to understand and master their environment. They discover whether or not the world is orderly and predictable and whether or not they can depend on others for support and caring. Those who are surrounded by love soon realize that they are competent and that they can have an impact on the world. This realization is confirmed when they see that their actions are treasured and encouraged, when adults are delighted by what they do, and when love is reflected in their eyes. As new brain research validates, quality interactions between adults and children in the early years establish the potential for later learning.

Traditional Lines Are Limiting ~ In traditional child care relationships, parents and caregivers relate to one another because of and through the child. Adult conversation is limited to events in each child's life—Ben's day, Ellie's naps, Jessica's play, Nick's stage of development, Hannah's friends, Chesere's setbacks, Chris's achievements. Regular exchanges of information between adults help maintain the continuity and appropriateness of care.

Some adults go beyond child-related information and bend the traditionally accepted line for service-based relationships. Like Beth and Rosie, they engage in conversations that help them get to know one another, value each other's point of view, and eventually treasure their relationship. Conversations spiral comfortably from topic to topic. They talk about their families of origin, reactions to world events, shared memories, personal values, and life choices. In the course of a given year, as they move together through events, they might discuss marriage, pregnancy, job loss, sickness, car accidents, friends who are visiting, divorce—the kind of rich and varied information people normally exchange when they are developing ties of friendship. As feelings of mutuality develop, they become freer to give each other advice, invite each other to social gatherings, and swap child care after hours for each other's children.

These personal interactions, shared experience, and accompanying feelings of bondedness weave the adults into a circle of caring. Whether it lasts only as long as the caregiving arrangement or for a lifetime, these circles offer a level of connection that cannot be realized in any other way. As friendships grow, parents become more trusting of providers, caregivers feel more supported by parents, and the children learn what it means to be part of an authentic community. They become active participants in a loving circle of people who care deeply about them, about the group, and about one another.

Bonding Needs Vary ~ It takes time, energy, commitment, and a willingness to overlook awkward situations to develop and sustain close relationships between adults in the child care setting. Even in ideal circumstances, these interactions can be a minefield.

Parents normally experience guilt, jealousy, role confusion, stress, and fear of loss when they entrust their children to the care of others. Many set up defenses to deal with this emotional rollercoaster. According to T. Berry Brazelton, in an address at the 1991 National Center for Clinical Infant Programs Conference, parents deal with the stress of leaving children in a number of predictable ways. Denial is one of them. Parents may say: "It doesn't matter. She hardly knows I'm gone. Besides, she's bored when it's just the two of us at home." Focusing on trivial matters is another: "I would have no problem leaving my child, if you could just keep him clean!" Distressed parents also use detachment to cope with their pain: "Aren't you excited, honey? After work and day care, Mommy is going out and you are going to have Gina for a baby-sitter!" Gatekeeping—questioning the provider's abilities and experiences—is yet another way parents try to get by: "I know this child better than you do! He never cries when I put him down for a nap at home."

Defenses like these are difficult to break down, especially by caregivers who are busy erecting barriers of their own. Providers struggle with the pain of loving (and losing) other people's children. They know their attachments—no matter how intense—are likely to be short-lived. They worry about loving children too much and losing them when they move on. They fear that their relationships with children will be discounted and that their ties will be taken for granted. Many struggle with poor self-images, and consider themselves to be less important than those who have "real" jobs in the workforce. Low self-esteem causes providers to defer to parents who work outside the home, yet quietly resent the decisions made. None of this lends itself to investments in satisfying relationships.

Parents and providers must answer thorny questions if they want to overcome obstacles such as these. Working parents, especially those with infants and toddlers, must consider what is best for their children: If I choose a caregiver who develops close bonds with my preschooler, what can I do to ensure that family ties remain strong? Can I feel compassion for a caregiver who invests fully in what will probably be a short-term relationship with my child? Is it possible or even attractive to me to redesign my family circle to include a relative stranger?

Providers must question themselves as well: How important is it to me to have close relationships with every parent who has a child in care? Can I be comfortable with somewhat distant relationships with parents of infants and toddlers if this is what the adults prefer? Can I feel compassion for parents who feel guilty and afraid when they leave young children and go off to work? Can I be close to children during the day and yet let go at night, or when the arrangement ends?

The ways in which parents and providers answer these questions determine the nature of their relationships. Some parents will try to keep the responsibility for bonding within the family and prefer care with weaker emotional ties. They will choose caregivers who comfort children when they are unhappy, feed them when they are hungry, and help them relax when they are sleepy, but will not form close or lasting attachments. Parents who want their provider to develop stronger bonds to the children will work toward closer parent-provider relationships. As long as a child's need for bonding is understood, it doesn't matter which choice the parent makes. The important thing is that the child grows up securely attached to loving adults.

What Do Parent-Provider Relationships Look Like When They Go Beyond the Norm?

୬ **ALTHOUGH WE KNOW** that not all relationships in child care settings blossom into authentic friendships, deep long-lasting relationships can and do develop between adults who share the care. What happens to families when personal and professional lines are blurred? What problems are predictable? What are the benefits to children and families and to providers? What happens when the caregiving years are over? Parents and caregivers usually have much to say about their relationships with each other.

Providers Reach Out; Parents Reach Back ~ High-quality providers who thrive in the child care world are gifted in loving. They welcome parents into their hearts right along with the children. Willingly, they open their homes to strangers and live their lives in public. Veterans know intuitively that relationships are built through authentic sharing of selves, and most aren't afraid to do so—warts and all. "Family child care providers show their human side and [reveal] how [they] deal with real life, solve problems, cope and thrive," observes a trainer from Colorado.

This natural openness can be threatening to parents who are used to being reserved with strangers and are comfortable maintaining traditional "businesslike" distance in other parts of their lives. New parents can feel embarrassed to reveal their uncertainties and imperfections as they grow in experience. For that reason, providers, with their natural inclinations toward interpersonal sharing and bonding, make sure connections remain current and solid. They begin this process at the first interview when they tell parents that they need openness and honesty. They continue by screening for values—questioning parents about discipline, eating habits, toy weapons, and toilet training—testing the match to see if it has potential for real teamwork.

Quality providers continue the relationship-building process as long as children remain in care. They touch base at drop-off and pick-up times, asking questions and chatting about the children's days, the parents' days, and their own days as well. Sometimes they call at night to find out how sick children are doing, or to support families during upheavals or crises. They throw parties, organize potlucks, and set up yearly reunions with little thought to whether parents will reciprocate. They consider these efforts to be part of the job of developing and maintaining comfortable connections for families and take their extra social duties in stride.

Although some parents hold themselves back, many move beyond traditional roles and respond in reciprocal ways to providers, once the door is open. They talk about older children who are not in care, visits to grandparents, community events, and problems on the job. As relationships deepen, parents begin to keep track of events in their provider's life as well. They take an interest in her children, her life, the plants she's growing, classes she's taking, activities that she took part in over the weekend. They bring treats for holidays and send cards or gifts for special occasions.

For many parents and providers, ongoing social contacts evolve out of child care connections. At one provider's annual caroling party, two-thirds of the people who attended were past or current child care families, even though many others had been invited. She reported with amazement that "the majority of this crowd—jamming on rhythm instruments, singing 'Hakuna Matata' at the top of their lungs, and filling my house with joy—were former 'clients' who had quietly slipped themselves into the category of life friends."

Friendships Blossom with Contracts and Clear Policies ~ As noted earlier, most high-quality providers are committed to contracts and written policies as a means of establishing professionalism. This clarification of business procedures seems to be a critical factor in developing caring relationships as well. For example, a Georgia provider who was casual about her closing time had some parents who scooted out guiltily when they chatted for more than five or ten minutes, while others followed her into the kitchen to talk, long after her doors were closed and she was ready to cook dinner. "When I made it clear in my written policies that parents were welcome to hang around and enjoy time with me and with each other until 6:00, my closing time, they became much more reasonable about it. The same ones still stay until the last minute, but now they joke and nudge each other out the door when the clock strikes 6:00, 'so Azzie can have her life back'!"

In the collection of essays *Kinship and Communities: Families in America*, David M. Schneider points out that in the United States, kinships that are not determined by blood are usually set up and changed by group will. These agreements encourage mutual growth, unity, and a feeling of community. Policies and contracts serve as kinship agreements within the family child care setting. When trouble brews, the haven of contracts and policies can keep relationships functioning, as a provider from Georgia reveals:

"I took on two kids and a single mom who was just barely making it," she explains. "I gave her a discount and offered free school-age pick-up, trying to be supportive and helpful because she was a new friend and I saw how hard her life was. But as the months went on, her needs grew and grew—late pick-ups, extensions on payment, constant venting of her overwhelming problems. Every time I let a policy slide, she'd need more, and she didn't seem to notice she was pushing too far, even though I'd told her more than once.

"It became clear to me that her life had more crises than I could handle. I got overwhelmed, felt manipulated, and considered terminating her. But her children were happy and thriving—they were friends with my own—and I hated to turn them into latchkey kids. So the mom and I had a few hard talks and some good cries together. We agreed to try to go back to a more businesslike relationship and worked out a new stricter arrangement. To my surprise, she stopped the manipulative behaviors, and we finished out the year on a more constructive note than I would ever have imagined possible.

"We still know each other. We're not close—her life is still too hard—but we socialize now and then, and our kids still play together.

She even finds ways to do nice things for me, to sort of pay me back, I guess. My written policies really brought us both back to a place where we would work together, even if we couldn't be close friends."

Clarifying mutually accepted boundaries is part of any adult relationship. If expectations and limits are clear, everyone can relax and focus constructively on cooperation, or work toward termination. In family child care, clear policies and contracts are the boundaries. When boundaries are accepted, providers feel respected and supported by parents, and parents feel safe and cared for by providers. Over time, the trust that is built between them makes it possible for kinship and community to evolve.

Providers Go the Extra Mile... ~ It isn't widely publicized, but many parents and caregivers go off the scales in support of one another. Providers who are lucky enough to find parents who give back, or who are experienced enough to teach parents to do so, experience responsive and reciprocal relationships that make the child care connection a gift to everyone.

Many providers go to classes with parents, and even without them, to learn about children's special needs. They keep children for days on end when unstable parents are overwhelmed or disappear from view; they take children on weeknights or weekends to give single parents a break; and they allow parents to delay payment for weeks or even months during a crisis. They offer themselves to parents as birthing coaches, informal therapists, job-search networkers, chauffeurs, and marriage counselors. Some serve snacks at drop-off or pick-up times to give everyone time to relax together. They give presents on special occasions, invite families for holidays, organize birthday parties for the children, and sponsor yearly reunions. There are even caregivers who plan yearly camping trips and visits to theme parks as part of their services, at their own expense.

Some providers go the extra mile for the sake of the children, without knowing how their efforts will be received. "I was picking up children at school when the teacher told me, 'Val is falling down a lot. She isn't tripping over her shoes. She seems to be trying to draw attention to herself.' I knew the parents were having trouble with each other. The mother had asked me not to tell, but I felt that if the teacher knew, she would be more sympathetic to the child and would have a better idea of how to handle it.

"I told the teacher that Val's parents were having marital problems. Even though I was under confidentiality, I thought it was in the best interest of the child. I made a judgment call. And once I did that, the teacher's whole attitude changed." When the mother found out what the provider had done—and why she had done it— she was grateful.

A Georgia provider, who is a veteran of over twenty years, found herself in a similar situation. She was concerned about trespassing parental boundaries, but felt an equal sense of urgency on behalf of the child. She stepped outside the role she was paid for and, acting on her intuition and love for the child, set up a conference that included the teacher, the parents, the child, and herself. The risk she took could have turned out badly, but her bond to the family paid off and everyone benefited.

...And Parents Do Too ~ Providers are not the only ones who go the extra mile; parents give freely and generously as well. They offer flowers, garden harvests, and kind notes to caregivers, especially after challenging weeks. Some give presents and set up time off or surprise bonuses. Parental generosity runs the gamut from small simple gestures to large important ones. The stories are endless and delightful. One parent performed a surprise spruce-up of a provider's van. A group of low-income parents raised money so their providers could go on a family child care association retreat. A couple from Hawaii surprised their provider with an authentic island Christmas dinner, complete with roasted pig and pineapple boats. A provider from Michigan was treated to a shopping trip and a new suit by a parent who wanted to help celebrate her invitation to speak at a national conference. Many parents assist caregivers with their homes and their yards.

A Tennessee parent helped a provider who had a leak in her roof. "No one could figure out what was wrong," says the grateful provider. "[This father] worked out the configurations and made something [special] so the water could run off." The families of another provider planned a group cookout and repaired her fence as part of the event.

A Colorado parent motivated others in the group to show appreciation for their provider. "I decided Cathy needed a raise, so I stuck around one day at pick-up time, and I said to the other parents, 'I'm giving Cathy a raise.' Cathy said, 'What are you doing?' but I could tell she appreciated it."

Other parents come to the rescue when providers are sick. The families of more than one provider have taken days off and taken over her business and family life to cover emergencies. They take turns doing child care, cooking dinner, caring for the provider's children, and keeping the house clean until she can return to work.

One caregiver, who was too dizzy from the flu to work, tells a story about the parents of the children she cares for who were "not only supportive and understanding about the sick day, but one called to see if I needed anything from the store, another offered to take my own child for dinner, and a third appeared at my door with a jar of homemade chicken soup! I was amazed! I had never dared take a day off before; it almost made me want to be sick more often."

While parent support sometimes revolves around particular events, it also takes the form of ongoing involvement. A couple from Massachusetts helps their provider "as often as we can" to show their gratitude. "Michael is always fixing her car. We paid her for holidays before she even thought of it."

Amazingly enough, many parents insist on paying for holidays, even when providers don't request it. "I get paid for these days off, why shouldn't you?" They also rally behind providers who have hit hard times, sometimes at great personal investment. One provider moved an entire workshop group to tears telling her story. "When my husband died, I didn't call any of my former parents to tell them. It really didn't occur to me that they would want to know. On the day of the funeral, the church was packed! There were almost a hundred parents and children there. I don't know who started it; they all called each other. They didn't really know my husband, but they came to support me. They wanted me to know I was still loved."

Now and then, parents go out of their way to take on advocacy work that is important to their providers. "One of my parents was a writer," shares a caregiver from California. "She was the children's editor for the newspaper. She testified at hearings for family day care and talked about the importance of my work for her as her provider. Another time, the California Child Care Development Agency had parents and providers come in to talk about different kinds of child care. Family child care was up and coming. She came in to talk about how it worked for her."

There is also the story about a bold parent who helped her provider take a group of low-income children to Disneyland. The caregiver routinely drove her preschoolers there in her motor home for two or three days each year as a "graduation" treat. Usually parents paid or raised money to cover the cost, but this year they didn't do any fundraising and four low-income children couldn't pay their way. One of the mothers went to her boss to borrow the money. She told him about the caregiver and showed him the calendar of activities offered during the year. He was amazed and called the caregiver to ask some questions. When she asked who he was, he told her he was her "godfather." He told her that a mother had told him about her need and his firm had decided to donate the money she needed to take the four children on the trip.

Stories of parents and caregivers who have gone the extra mile for one another make it obvious that current thinking, which emphasizes the caregiver's responsibility for developing relationships without teaching parents to give back more than money, is missing the mark. Unbalanced give-and-take in a relationship exhausts the giver and increases guilt in the taker, without anyone's knowing why. Inequality only works in adult-child relationships, which remain stratified until children grow up and balance the scales. The limited fee-for-service model often leaves parents feeling vaguely uneasy and providers resentful and burnt out.

On the other hand, reciprocal behavior brings feelings of well-being and a sense of fulfillment on both sides of the relationship. Parents and caregivers who respond to personal needs and go the extra mile for one another experience the magic that opens between strangers who learn to be friends. The kinship that evolves has an important impact on the lives of the children they share.

Bonds Often Last a Lifetime ~ Caregivers and parents spend a year or two or even more sharing their lives and the ups and downs of raising children; it should be no surprise that feelings of friendship and kinship grow between them. It makes sense that people who spend so much time together will become connected and help each other out. When the taboos of tradition are laid aside and connections—

even those with former strangers—are allowed to blossom, who would let them go permanently?

Most providers have relationships with at least a few families that have stood the test of time. Special parents take time to send holiday cards and pictures and make regular calls to keep caregivers

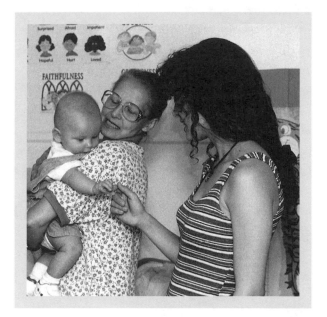

informed about their grown-up "babies." Parents have been known to invite providers to weddings of children who still consider them "extra moms" because family bonds have lasted over the years. More than one provider has been asked to work with children who have unexpectedly turned into "incorrigible teens." Several have taken teenagers in as foster children, at the parent's request and to everyone's benefit. Surprising as it may seem to some, stories about long-term connections between providers and child care families are not few and far between. For veteran providers from every possible background, this is the norm!

Reunions with providers can bring fascinating nuggets of memory to the surface. "I remember wanting to use the big potty because I hated to make Liza have to clean out that little potty all the time," one young teen told her former provider and her mother at a dinner they shared one night. Both adults were amazed. Neither one had had any idea why this child had made that decision at such an early age. Contact with this caregiver brought the experience back, and this time the child had words to describe her feelings and put it into perspective.

Over the long run, children of parents and caregivers who stay in touch are likely to be more secure and confident, even if the connections are spread out over the years. According to Ruthellen Josselson, author of *The Space Between Us: Exploring the Dimensions of Human Relationships*, when attachment figures are available and responsive, we feel secure, even though we may be unaware of the psychological hows and whys. Perceived loss of these figures can make us feel torn apart, as though our lives have come unraveled. It isn't the actual presence of attachment figures that gives us confidence, however. What really counts is their continued existence in our memories, their perceived accessibility, and our expectation that they will be responsive when we meet again.

Parents can keep good memories about child care providers alive for their children for years after the child care arrangement has ended. Those who also make an effort to stay in touch give children something extra beyond the basic child care experience. They offer the chance for children to cherish and maintain bonds that were deep and meaningful. These children do not have to wonder if they were loved by adults in their faded memories. They can see and feel for themselves that the strong arms that once held them still exist and are eager to hug them again. Connections like these are most likely to extend beyond the child care years when bonds go three ways: parent-child, provider-child, and parent-provider.

This important but illusive gift of confidence and emotional security for children rests on the parents' willingness to sustain child care bonds over time. While the caregiver typically initiates and encourages relationships with the parents, it is the parents who determine how much and how long they will reach back to the provider. Generally, it is the caring relationships that develop between parents and providers separate from the child that inspire parents to meet the attachment needs of their children and find ways for everyone to get together after child care ends.

New Family Circles Develop Community Webs ~ The significance of parent-provider relationships is best understood against the backdrop of family and community life today. The neighborhoods many of us knew as children are gone. Few of today's youngsters have the opportunity—or the freedom—to troop in and out of their own homes, much less those of the neighbors, the way many of us did when we were young. Today, the children next door aren't at home; they're in child care. And their parents, not to mention nearly everyone else who lives on the street, are working. The notion of children playing unsupervised in the neighborhood or walking alone to friends' houses is becoming a thing of the past.

Changes in the workforce have transformed family life. In 1988, according to a Louis Harris survey cited by Richard Louv in

Childhood's Future (15), the average work week was 46.8 hours. Professional people worked a weekly average of 52.2 hours. Leisure time shrunk proportionately, from 26.2 hours per week in 1973 to 16.6 hours in 1987—a 37 percent drop in the amount of time we relaxed, played, or spent time with our families. Most parents worked long hours, with little time to relax or play with their children. There is no doubt that the workload in the furure will be as high or higher.

Working parents are starved for time and feel isolated from other families. Most have their hands full holding a job, picking up and dropping off children at child care, cooking, washing dishes, shopping, running errands, and washing clothes. Extended families

don't offer the same level of involvement and support they used to, either. Grandparents often live far away; brothers, sisters, aunts, uncles, and cousins don't necessarily keep in touch. Working parents have little time to sit over a cup of coffee and talk with other adults about their troubles or exchange bits of advice. Friendship is a luxury many can't afford.

Close parent-provider relationships are helping to fill the holes and gaps that have been torn in family and community life. Friendly conversation at the end of the day eases the alienation and stress that parents feel after working under pressure on fixed deadlines. Small talk at pick-up time provides a transition that helps parents return to the life of the family. Veteran caregivers offer parents a sounding board to test out new ideas for discipline and behavior management. Parents and providers who care join together to celebrate children's milestones and accomplishments.

Richard Louv predicts that the time will come when we view child care as a part of a larger family and community web. He believes that when this happens, quality will come to mean what is good for the family, rather than what is good solely for the child or what is good for the employer. This time has already come for children and families in high-quality family child care settings.

Child Care Becomes "Guilt-Lite" ~ Parents who experience child care as a circle of love gradually feel a lessening of their burdens of worry and guilt. Their children are no longer "just put somewhere" during the day; they are entrusted to kin-like friends who have come to care deeply about them and about their families as well. Parents see that their children are surrounded with an envelope of love that inspires self-esteem, creativity, responsiveness, generosity, love, and a joy of life. They know that they are part of a community, a nucleus of people who care about one another.

Little by little, in the soothing warmth of these relationships, the pain of guilt eases. Parents are less preoccupied when they are away from their children and less influenced by feelings of remorse

and wrongdoing when they are together. Free of nagging self-criticism and doubt, they are more able to enjoy their children with simple delight.

Parent-caregiver bonds reduce inner conflict for providers too. This freedom is reflected in their attitudes toward families and the level of care offered to children. Providers who are bonded to families feel supported in their choice of work and nurtured by relationships. Their contentment expresses itself in greater attunement and responsiveness to children and a greater commitment to professional, high-quality programs. They are willing to stay in the business longer; it is easier for them to cope with the daily disturbances, conflicts, and disruptions that are an inevitable part of the job. Authentic bonds with parents help providers become more resilient, more relaxed, and more understanding under pressure. In the words of one provider, "Genuine relationships with parents Is the piece that keeps on giving back."

Parents and caregivers who understand the importance of authentic relationships know that they have achieved the best care possible for children of working families. They are participants in the joy human beings experience everywhere when they live and work together within a circle of love.

The New Family-Circle Design Benefits Everyone

꒦ **THOSE WHO ARE INVOLVED** in designing new family circles, based on authentic relationships between parents and providers, will have an impact on community life fifty years from now. The children in child care today are tomorrow's parents and our workforce of the future. The relationships they observe and experience are the models they will use for their own adult lives, just as we rely on the models that were used by the families who raised us.

The circle as a model of relationship in quality child care blends the best of the world of friendship with the best of the world of commerce. It enables parents to feel comfortable with the child care arrangements they have chosen and makes caregivers feel supported by the families they serve. Children are surrounded with loving bonds and attachments that will impact them for a lifetime.

Although they are in evidence in all kinds of family child care homes, the value of these small circles is not widely understood, even by families and caregivers who participate in them. The field of early childhood generally stresses the business side of care and warns against the dangers of too much informality in child care settings. Providers hide their love for children and regard friendships with parents as desirable but not a necessary component of quality care. Parents downplay their relationships with providers, regarding those friendships as personal "strokes of luck."

Our inability to recognize the importance of these relationships stems, in part, from our conflicted feelings about child care. Quality care produces painful paradoxes. Even when they know that their very young children need to be with adults who love them, caring and well-meaning parents feel anxious when providers show deep affection. They see the value of their children loving the adults who care for them, and yet they feel uneasy when they witness strong child-caregiver attachments between their children and people who,

not long ago, were strangers. They sense that the distance and reserve that works for adults may be damaging to children in child care, and yet a part of them wants just that.

If we look at the whole picture—children's needs, parental needs, parental fears, caregiver needs, caregiver fears—we know how important parent-provider relationships are in the lives of children and their families. Parents who have close relationships with their children's providers permit child-caregiver bonds to flourish. It is that simple. Those who are busy creating genuine parent-provider relationships have the potential to reweave the tears caused by rapid social change in today's world. By redesigning the family circle and creating new communities of people who care about one another, these pioneering adults are designing a new model of "guilt-lite," quality child care.

It is time to step back and acknowledge the part that caring parent-provider relationships play in the lives of children and quality child care. Educators, parents, and caregivers can begin the process by working to remove social taboos against the bonds that grow in child care. We can teach the value of good matches and the importance of deeper connections. We can help parents and providers reach for a comfortable balance between their personal and business lives, between friendships and formal arrangements. Ultimately, we can include parent-caregiver relationships in the equation when we calculate the elements of quality care. Our work is cut out for us.

Chapter 5

Ring the bells that still can ring.

Forget your perfect offering.

There's a crack in everything.

That's how the light gets in.

~ Leonard Cohen

A Quiet Crisis

"YOU'LL DO WHAT I SAY AND YOU'LL DO IT NOW!" ~ *It's 11:30 a.m. and four-year-old Jason is absorbed in building a block structure in a corner of the living room. At the other end, eighteen-month-old Jenny and the two-year-old twins are struggling over a musical toy. When the quarrel crescendos into pushing and tears, Rita slams her magazine down on the coffee table and intervenes.*

"That's enough!" she says with exasperation. "It's time for lunch." Roughly she separates the children, puts the toy on the TV, and pulls the twins into the kitchen. Jenny toddles behind, snuffling unhappily. "You, too, Jason," the care-giver calls over her shoulder. "Put those blocks away; it's time for lunch."

Jason doesn't appear to hear her. He continues adding blocks to his building. Rita sits the younger children in their chairs and comes back to where Jason is playing. Surprised to see her, he looks up, "I'm building a television station, like on Mr. Rogers," he explains.

"It's lunchtime. I already told you. Put those blocks away."

Jason looks hurt and confused.

"Now! I'm waiting!"

Silently, passively, shoulders sagging, Jason begins to dismantle his half-finished creation.

"That's good. There's no more time for block play today. You'll be going down for a nap as soon as lunch is over. Now come on! The girls are waiting!"

Jason obeys without comment. He has learned better than to argue.

⚜

Connie is pouring coffee for her neighbor, who has stopped by to return a borrowed video. Two-year-old Tanya is curious and comes into the kitchen to find out what's going on.

"This doesn't have anything to do with you," Connie tells her sharply. "You can turn right around and go back into the living room and play."

Tanya hovers uncertainly near the doorway.

"You heard me! Go on now! Go play!" Connie commands, turning back to the neighbor. "She's such a little busybody!"

Surprised at the tone and at the adult laughter turned in her direction, Tanya looks like she is about to cry.

"Gonna cry about it, are you? Then you can sit right there until we're through talking. Right there." She points to a spot in the doorway. "And you can sit there until I say you can get up."

Tanya obeys. She puts her thumb in her mouth and waits, sniffling quietly. The women turn back to their personal business, forgetting she is there.

⚜

Three-year-old Mollie arrives at child care in tears. She misses her mother, who has gone out of town on a business trip. Erica comforts Mollie as long as her father is in the house. When he leaves, she puts Mollie on the floor in the hallway, tells her to pull herself together, and walks away.

Mollie spends thirty minutes sobbing and then whimpering. Gradually, she becomes calm enough to get up and join the other children for circle time. She has

nearly reached the group when she trips over a stuffed bear. Her eyes fill again
with tears and she reaches expectantly toward Erica who is reading a book
to the rest of the children.

"You've been looking for attention all morning, Mollie. You aren't the
only child in this house, you know! I can't hold you all day. You just have to
get used to it."

The tears spill over. Mollie's sobbing resumes.

"You're not hurt. You're just spoiled. Now sit down! Everybody's waiting."

The Crisis of Substandard Care

The behavior of these caregivers is more common than most people would like to admit. They aren't being intentionally mean or unfeeling; in all likelihood, they don't even realize they are doing anything wrong. Their focus is on what works for the adult and for the group. Given the stresses and demands of their work, and limited by lack of training and personal worth, they are unable—or unwilling—to imagine the world through the eyes of their individual young charges. Jason's block project has no importance when lunch and nap are the goals; Tanya's curiosity intrudes on adult needs for companionship; Mollie's sadness is a nuisance at circle time. Whether through ignorance or callousness, these providers, and others like them, are unresponsive to children's feelings and insensitive to their experience.

Up to this point, this book has celebrated the accomplishments of professional family child care providers who offer quality care to children of working families. Actual words of providers and parents from every region of the country and every income level have shown that high-quality family child care providers care deeply about the children entrusted to them and about their families as well. Their stories challenge child care advocates to look beyond traditional norms to a new hope-filled approach to child care, one that does a better job of meeting the needs of young children. They make it clear that even in situations where caregivers and parents meet as strangers, child care relationships can—and do—develop ties that benefit everyone.

But now it is time to look at the bigger picture. According to the Children's Foundation's 1996 *Family Child Care Licensing Study*, there are approximately 300,000 regulated providers and approximately one million informal caregivers in the United States. Although many offer excellent loving care, many also offer care that is unprofessional and minimally acceptable. In *The Study of Children in Family Child Care and Relative Care*, Ellen Galinsky and her colleagues interviewed 820 mothers and 226 providers in three urban areas. Only 9 percent of the caregivers were rated as good, 35 percent scored in the inadequate range, and 56 percent were judged to provide custodial care only. Although the sample was small, this

report substantiates what many have long suspected. Large numbers of children are receiving substandard care. The potential for harm increases every year as more and more children enter child care at younger and younger ages.

Substandard care manifests itself in many different ways. It can appear in the form of unsanitary health practices and hazardous conditions: food that has been prepared or stored improperly, hands that are rarely washed, and stairways without gates to protect curious infants and toddlers. Homes can lack stimulating toys, books, and age-appropriate learning materials. They can be over-enrolled, dominated by TV, or operated like holding tanks until parents return.

The most heart-wrenching settings are those where children are made to feel unimportant and unlovable. Care that is adult-focused or nonempathetic is the hardest to detect. In some cases, providers keep their selfishness or negative attitudes hidden from everyone except for the children. In others, distancing or belittling behaviors are not seen as problems by parents because they are too busy to notice, feel trapped by lack of choices, or approach their own children in a similar manner. Parents with limited experience tend to miss the subtle evidence of emotional abuse, even when it is out in the open, especially if the children do not complain.

Findings in *The Study of Children in Family Child Care and Relative Care* regarding caregiver-child attachments and the emotional needs of children are alarming: "Overall, 50 percent of the children in this sample are securely attached, 34 percent have anxious/avoidant relationships, and 16 percent have anxious/resistant relationships with their providers" (78). Although half of the children in this study were comfortable with their providers, the others spent most of their days with people they disliked, or, worse, feared. One-half was thriving, but the rest were learning lessons of survival: how to cope and protect themselves against intrusions of others; how to survive insensitive invasions of self; how to deal with uncaring adults who claim to have children's interests at heart, but don't. Nearly 400 children were learning, day by day, to doubt their own competence and self-worth.

Negative Experiences Teach Negative Patterns ~ Children pattern their interactions on the formative relationships they have with adults. Young children, especially infants and toddlers, learn from the way adults interact with them—how they talk to them, hold them, feed them, respond to their cries, play with them, pick them up, and lay them down. They learn from tones of voice—sing-song, babbling, anger, laughter, questions, surprise. They learn from the quality of touch—gentle rocking, playful tickling, loving hugs. And they learn from the way adults look into their eyes. The nuances of spontaneous, everyday interactions teach children the emotional difference between connections and distance, consistency and rigidity, honesty and faking it.

Positive exchanges teach young children what it is like to be taken seriously, to be understood and to have an effect on other people. Children learn how to be partners and discover the give-and-take of relationships where each person matters. Children who have been loved and nurtured most of the time learn to love and nurture others most of the time. They learn to listen and respond with compassion and empathetic feelings. They become willing to resolve conflicts, account for differences, and prevent disagreements from spiraling. Because grownups have set the example, they develop patience and learn how to take others seriously.

In like manner, negative interactions with adults teach young children about relationships in which people are viewed as objects. In these contacts, give-and-take are off balance and selfish manipulation is practiced without regard for the needs or feelings of others. Children who are told repeatedly through words and actions that responsiveness is unimportant and that they are disruptive, underfoot, or a nuisance learn to believe that this is true. They learn about powerlessness, emptiness, and the absence of personal worth. Following patterns of alienation and abuse that they learn in the formative years, they are predisposed to alienate and abuse others.

Neglect Damages Self-Esteem ~ Young children who are abandoned emotionally often develop characteristics that distinguish them from others their age. Preschoolers who have spent most of their time with loving adults tend to be open, exploratory, experimenting, questioning, and full of curiosity. By the age of four or five, they are able to play constructively alone or with others, with minimal supervision. If a grownup appears who is not a family member or kin-like friend, children generally ignore the newcomer and continue with their own agendas.

On the other hand, children who are consistently ignored or demeaned are always on the lookout for adults who will care about them and show interest in their lives. These children work aggressively and continuously for attention, even from total strangers. While most preschoolers tend to be shy or reserved around unknown adults, saving emotional appeals for those who care deeply about them, children who have been neglected rush up to every new adult who enters the room with appeals to be held, to be chosen, to be noticed. They don't differentiate between a smiling stranger and adults who love them because these children haven't discovered a difference. They are so desperate for love, it doesn't matter who the potential attention-giver may be. They quickly abandon their own activities and barrel over one another in an effort to be recognized in any way possible, even if it is negative.

Young children who are deprived of deep attachments to adults who are consistent generally end up regarding all adults as objects. In *Every Child's Birthright*, Selma Fraiberg found that the long-term ability to attach is impaired in varying degrees depending on the severity of the deprivation. Children who are consistently ignored typically enter into interchangeable relationships based solely on the ability of the other person to meet their needs, without a thought to the unique or special qualities of these partners, long-term connections, or the give-and-take of authentic relationships. They become teens and then adults who have little to give to others. Poor relationships in early life usually cause problems that last into adulthood and then are passed along.

Child Care Is Shaping Tomorrow's Society ~ A generation ago, young children learned about themselves and relationships with others through interactions with parents, close family members, and kin-like friends. The mothers, fathers, or grandparents who spent the days feeding them, rocking them, and singing them to sleep were also the ones who taught the children about themselves and the possibilities

of love and relationship. For increasing numbers of children today, lessons about love and relationship are also learned through interactions with paid providers who have no family ties or connections.

More than half of the infants and toddlers in the United States spend as much as nine to eleven hours a day, five days a week, fifty weeks a year with strangers who may or may not grow to love them and nurture them as their own. Provider-child interactions are influencing children's views of themselves and setting patterns for interactions with others. They are shaping today's society and that of the future. Whether society pays attention to them or not, caregiver-child interactions are already playing a large role in the well-being of millions of children. And the number of children impacted by this giant social experiment is growing every year.

Despite the importance of child-caregiver interactions, and despite their influence during the child's formative years, little is done to ensure that those who provide child care are equipped to do a good job of creating healthy relationships with children and their families. On some level, we are still operating under the illusion that, like parenting, just about anyone who wants this job can do it.

When providers become state regulated, they are not screened for styles of interacting with children. In states where training is mandated, issues of health and safety are more likely to be addressed than program development or child-caregiver interactions. Training that does focus on relationship issues is more likely to use elementary schools or businesses rather than the home or family as models for relationships with children and families. Typically, caregivers are encouraged to keep things "businesslike" and to look at parents as clients or customers rather than members of their extended families.

Frustrating though it may be, the search for high-quality care is often a matter of luck. Agencies across the country help parents locate child care settings, but they make referrals, not recommendations, because they rightly believe that parents must make final judgments about the nurturing qualities of individual providers. All too often, however, parents are not in a position to make this determination. Consumer education is not advanced, guilt and jealousy cloud judgments, and choices are limited. Many parents simply have no idea how to go about assessing the emotional climate of a child care setting. Some are first-time parents and uncertain about child-rearing themselves. Some have grown up in families with unhealthy relationships and are unclear about what they should want. Others turn inappropriately for guidance to the first clear memories of their own experiences outside the home—usually those of second or third grade—making relationship issues seem unimportant. Even discerning parents who do have the ability to make reasonable assessments of child care providers may hit barriers. Often they do not have enough time nor the opportunity to know what a provider is like when she is alone with the children. Most cannot get around the limiting realities of affordability and availability of care.

The Crisis Is Growing

FAMILY INSTABILITY, ignorance, and poverty compound problems caused by substandard care. In 1994, the Carnegie Corporation of New York published a report titled *Starting Points: Meeting the Needs of Our Youngest Children.* The document reported the following:

✦ Of the 12 million children under the age of three in the United States today, a staggering number are affected by one or more risk factors that make healthy development more difficult.

✦ Almost one-fourth of families with children under three live in poverty, in unsafe neighborhoods, with poor access to quality child care, health services, or family support groups.

✦ Between 1987 and 1991, the number of children in foster care jumped by more than 50 percent.

✦ By 1993, almost one-half of all children could expect to experience a divorce during childhood and live an average of five years in a single-parent family.

✦ One in three victims of physical abuse is a baby. Almost 53 percent of the children who died of abuse or neglect in 1990 were less than one year old. (4)

Unhealthy conditions affecting children cut across every region, every ethnic group, and every income level. In all parts of society— economically affluent or depressed, urban, suburban, or rural—children live in dysfunctional homes, single-parent homes, and foster homes without the support that can be found in extended families or quality child care. Everywhere, children in the United States are exposed to the hostility and confusion of family separation, divorce, inadequate health care, physical abuse, emotional abuse, sexual abuse, and neglect.

The negative impact of these early experiences on individual children and on society can be staggering. Problems that originate in early childhood do not stop once the child reaches school age; they manifest themselves in one way or another throughout a person's lifetime. Children who spend most of their time with adults who are emotionally detached or indifferent usually wind up with problems in the classroom. They are easily distracted and frustrated, impulsive, and disruptive. They have difficulty following instructions, concentrating on written work, or respecting their classmates. They walk when they should be sitting, run when they should be walking, and leap off of things without knowing for sure where they will land. Their friendships are fractious. Minor disagreements and frustrations lead quickly to tears, accusations, and physical violence.

Sensitive to differences, children with emotional difficulties know that they don't get along well with other children. ("No one likes me!") They are aware that they try the patience of their teachers. ("She thinks I'm bad.") Although they may desperately want things to work, they just don't know how. Successful interactions with others feel about as reachable as the stars.

According to the 1992 report *Heart Start: The Emotional Foundations of School Readiness* : "In some states, close to one out of five children are required to repeat first grade. Many of them, unable to respond to any but the most ideal teaching conditions, then fall further and further behind. Often they become more discouraged, more withdrawn, more resentful and, in some cases, more disruptive with each grade" (3).

These patterns and responses continue through the teen years and on into adulthood. The same forces that made it hard for youngsters to form close friendships, set meaningful priorities, or persevere against obstacles continue to shape their lives. They have ongoing problems creating realistic goals, living up to responsibilities, translating feelings into words, and acknowledging the needs of others. Emotionally troubled or challenged individuals have difficulty following instructions, performing well on the job, and resolving interpersonal conflicts peacefully and reasonably.

The cost of failing to provide high-quality early childhood experiences for all of our children, no matter where they spend their time, is great—and everyone pays. Society pays in the form of more classrooms for children with "special needs," larger prisons, bigger police forces, more sophisticated means of surveillance, and more social programs. Families pay in fear for their well-being on city streets and for their children's futures. They pay in worry about taxes, the staggering cost of social programs, and the loss of safety nets like Medicare and Social Security. When so many are at risk, everyone is touched, if not now, then in generations to come.

New Starting Points

↗ **GIVEN THE CONDITION** of children and families in the United States, it is clear that we must revise our thinking on central child care issues. With the rising numbers of working parents and the role child care already plays in this crisis, child care must be addressed as both part of the problem and part of the solution. First, and most important, we must take a deeper look at attachments in the child care setting. Provider-child relationships must be viewed in terms of the child's emotional needs, particularly the needs of those who are very young. The natural inclination of providers and children to bond must be supported; close parent-caregiver relationships must be valued as well.

It's time to reappraise current models of child care, turn from models that put infants and toddlers at risk, and place the well-being of children over tradition. The benefits of the "new family circle" must be acknowledged, understood, and promoted. We have to recognize that quality care supports the needs of the whole family and work together to make it so.

Look at Love from a Child's Perspective ~ When we look at relationships in the child care setting, we must consider the child's perspective as well as the adult's: *What do children need from relationships in order to thrive? What impact do provider-child attachments have on a child's growth and development? Are there any situations in which attachments have a negative effect on the child? How do child care relationships impact children from single-parent households or families in turmoil? Do ethnic backgrounds make a difference?*

The questions are very different when parents are the focus: *Will my child love me if he goes to child care? Will she love me if she loves her caregiver, too? Can I afford quality care?*

For providers, issues revolve around professional status and personal standing: *How can I maintain a professional distance from children in care and still do a good job? Is it professional to get emotionally involved with my clients? Where do I draw the line? Will they still pay me if we get to be like family?*

These questions are important and worthy of further research. Studies like the 1996 project conducted by the National Institute of Child Health and Development Early Child Care Network, which explored the impact of child care on parent-child bonds, have begun to address deep parental concerns. But studies like these should not obscure the importance of the child's perspective. Caregiver-child attachments are also important to children in care, particularly for those who are very young or have special needs.

As child advocates, we must learn to put ourselves in the young child's shoes. Imagine how it might be to find that the first people you have come to love and trust are suddenly absent for most of every day. Imagine how you would feel to be picked up by strange arms, surrounded by new smells, and addressed by the unfamiliar voice of someone you do not know. Imagine how it would be to spend five days a week, nine hours a day, with someone who has cool or lukewarm feelings toward you. Now imagine how you would feel if you were with a caregiver who really cares about whether you are wet or dry, busy or bored, happy or frustrated, hungry or sleepy. Imagine her as someone who approaches you with joy and love in her eyes.

From the child's perspective, there can be no doubt that providers have a major impact on day-to-day life. When loving family members are not available, those who take their place become important to a child, whether the place they hold is recognized by others or not. The long-term effects of child care relationships have yet to be thoroughly studied and documented, but it's easy to understand how much caregivers count if you look at them through the eyes of a child.

Revise Traditional Child Care Models ~ Fee-for-service business models and those based on grade school programs do not serve the needs of very young children. In these approaches, the emphasis is on tasks and accomplishments, professionalism, and service goals rather than on the qualitative give-and-take of human connections and love. The rule of thumb is to restrict relationships to well-defined limits; clients are kept at a distance, with little room for attachments.

The fee-for-service business model is based on the assumption that the provider is paid to meet the basic custodial needs of the customer's children: changing diapers, wiping runny noses, feeding meals and snacks, putting out toys for play, and making sure that everyone has a nap. The custodial provider is not hired to teach children about the pleasure of exchanging joyful glances or about the pain of withdrawal and withholding love. Service is restricted to food, clothing, rest, cleanliness, and safety. Personal involvement with individual children or families, emotional investment in accomplishments or troubles, and long-term attachments simply are not part of the arrangement.

Overlaid on the business model is that of the elementary school classroom. Here, too, the provider is expected to maintain emotional distance from children and families. The emphasis is on cognitive development; teaching is the order of the day. Basic concepts, the alphabet, spatial relationships, numbers, colors, shapes, weather, days of the week, and traditional holidays are the curriculum, not trust or love.

These models may work for older preschoolers, especially those who have ample opportunity to meet their relational needs through family members and kin-like friends. But they do not work for infants and toddlers who are learning about themselves and their relationship to others during every moment of their waking hours. Children at this age should be with caregivers who are sensitive to their developmental needs and who are willing and able to give them their full attention.

Very young children and those with exceptional needs require providers who will teach them what they need to know about love, responsiveness, trust, hope, openness, and joy—as well as cognitive learning—in a safe and healthy environment. These elements are traditionally found in a high-quality home environment and a loving family. The home and family must be the model for out-of-home care. Anything less threatens normal growth and development.

Support Provider-Child Bonds

⬿ **THE INSTINCTIVE AFFECTION** that many providers feel for young children is similar to the feelings that most parents have for their offspring. The urge to shelter and protect the very young is innate, natural, and not confined to our own children. Most adults feel protective instincts when they hear an infant sobbing in a supermarket or see a young child running alone in a parking lot. Parental feelings bubble up when we hold friends' babies against our shoulders, enjoying the warmth of newborn skin against our cheeks, inhaling the perfume of downy soft hair. If nothing else, these feelings are nature's way of assuring us that our species will continue, grow, and thrive.

A child's instinct to reciprocate love is also innate. Children are born ready to respond to loving gestures; without any coaching, they feel happiness when they share joy with others. They smile and light up with pleasure when parents coo or laugh and play with them; they respond just as enthusiastically to others who single them out to giggle or play or snuggle together over a story. Intuitively, they know the rightness of sharing and reciprocating love.

Bonds that develop between young children and their caregivers are the natural outcome of human instinct, familiarity, love, and gentle nurturing. Attachments deepen with time, as the caregiver is able to recognize the individual needs of each child and respond authentically to them. And yet, many providers and parents have come to believe that caregiver-child attachments are an embarrassment, a trespass across boundaries that should be off-limits to nonfamily members. Often without thought, they support social taboos against strangers, limit interactions to kin, and put their children's emotional development at risk.

When parents or child care educators express disapproval or reservations about caregiver-child attachments, providers usually pull back, hide their feelings, and adjust to the expectations of those who seem to know better. Reluctant to challenge this powerful societal taboo, they begin to distrust their natural inclinations to bond and become more self-conscious and more removed. Their delight in each child's development becomes more detached and distant. Interactions with the children become cooler, less spontaneous, and more custodial in nature. Gradually, relationships are colored by the image projected from those in judgment; and provider burnout is usually close behind.

On the other hand, when parents and trainers support the naturally loving attachments that develop in child care, the provider feels freer to invest more completely in each child's development. She feels empowered to get to know each child better and to respond more quickly to individual frustrations and demands rather than standardize her approach to all children and families. In short, when parents and society sanction caregiver-child attachments, the provider is able to treat each child like one of her own. And that's what's good for the children.

We no longer have the luxury of pretending that intimate interactions with young children can be contained within the genetic circle. Child care is here to stay, and child care in the United States is

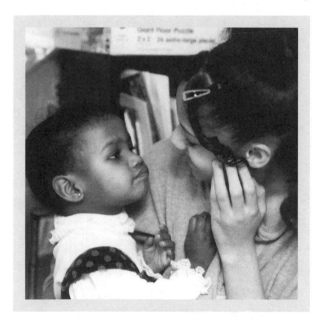

in the hands of strangers. It's time for us to view parental feelings and genuine attachments between providers and young children as indicators of quality rather than the result of imbalance or misjudgment. To maintain traditional social taboos against loving other people's children is to put our future as a loving species, not to mention the capability of individual children to learn and thrive, at risk.

We must acknowledge that caregiver-child bonds play an important role in child development and support caregivers in their natural inclinations to form close attachments. We must help children develop the trust and courage they need to explore and participate in the world of relationships, without the fear of loyalty conflicts between parents and providers. Our work will be well-rewarded with generations of adults who know how to form responsible and responsive relationships, and how to pass that knowledge on.

Encourage Parent-Provider Relationships ~ The very nature of caregiver-child relationships rests on the strength and frequency of authentic connections between the adults who share each child. When parents and providers go beyond the norm in their interactions, the friendships that result are more than a fringe benefit. These ties give caregiver-child bonds their depth, stability, and durability. They are the cornerstone of quality care.

When parent-provider relations are distant, adults tend to view themselves as competitors, rather than partners in care. This reserve, coupled with traditional societal attitudes and the guilt parents feel about leaving their children, cause parents to see caregivers as people who are incapable of holding any other kind of job. They discount the skills and talents required to care for other people's children. Similar forces cause providers to criticize parents for choosing material wealth over parenting and accuse them of abandoning their children. Attitudes like these that lock parents and providers into stilted, adversarial roles serve no one. Inevitably, the child-caregiver relationship suffers.

The only cure for this disease of the spirit is the development of genuine relationships between parents and caregivers that are based on mutual respect and a good match of values and expectations. Strong parent-caregiver partnerships are called for, with clear, honest communication, a commitment to work out problems as they appear, and a collaborative view of the role each adult plays in the child care setting. Daily contact and the casual exchange of personal lives are also part of the equation. Parents, providers, and child care advocates must work together to identify the contribution each adult makes to a child's well-being. Children are ready to teach us that all the adults in their lives are equally worthy of love. It's time for us to develop new and more flexible definitions for adult relationships in this setting so everyone can thrive.

Promote the Benefits of the Family-Circle Model ~ In a diverse society such as ours, the family-circle model of child care will not be the answer for everyone. Children's needs, the amount of time and energy each adult has to give, the availability of other family members, and ongoing personal commitments all play a part in determining whether or not the family-circle model is appropriate in a particular situation. In each family child care setting, some adults will maintain a respectful distance, some will go the extra mile for one another in the spirit of teamwork, and others will go beyond the norm to form lasting friendships.

Parents and daily caregivers who include one another in expanded family circles enable children to experience relationships with adults as seamless; everyone cares about everyone else. It is easy and natural for providers to offer parents extra support because there are ways for parents to give back. Relationships are authentic, reciprocal, and responsive.

These new family circles allow children to participate in small, caring communities where love flows not just to them, but back and forth between adults as well. Children learn the essence of kinship and the security of loving care in much the same way children do in well-functioning extended families. They witness their parents and providers offering help to one another without reserve, taking time to do small, nourishing favors.

Children observe their parents writing notes and thanking providers with flowers for their patience after a challenging week. They see them bringing a present for the provider's child on her birthday, making chicken soup when everyone is sick, or offering help in the form of roof repairs, playground maintenance, plumbing, wiring, gardening, splitting firewood—just because they can.

Children see their providers strengthen friendships with parents in equally caring and reciprocal ways: sending home a casserole with a parent who is under the weather, offering to keep a child overnight so his parents can take some time alone, putting together a travel kit for a child who is taking her first airplane trip, sharing food from the garden that everyone has helped tend, understanding when a parent is running late because of a surprise meeting, mentoring and assisting parents whose lives are in crisis.

For those who work at it, the rewards of developing an expanded family circle in the child care setting can be great. Children have a chance to bask in the love that surrounds them while they learn critical lessons about the give-and-take of adult relationships. Parents feel less pain and guilt when they are at work because they know that their children are with people who have become part of their own circles of caring; mutual trust and respect transform feelings of loss and regret.

This same trust and respect, coupled with supportive appreciation, bolsters providers as well. Caregivers feel sustained by relationships with parents as they contend with the inevitable upsets and trying behaviors of children in care. They stay in business as much for the connections they have with the parents as they do for love of the children.

Everyone thrives when children are part of a loving circle. Child and family advocates must help working parents look at their child care arrangements with this in mind. Early childhood professionals must help adults free themselves of the fears and societal taboos toward sharing children and open themselves to the development of authentically caring relationships, even when everyone begins as strangers. Parents must be taught how to give more than money in return for the loving care their families receive from providers.

When parents, children, and caregivers care about one another, we all benefit—the family of today as well as the family of tomorrow. Those who have been nurtured and cared for by adults who care about one another will grow up ready to accept the responsibility of helping and nurturing others. The models they took part in when they were young will be the ones they will build on in the future. For those who already spend a majority of their days in loving child care settings and for those who follow, the future looks bright.

Chapter 6

Small things done consistently

in strategic places create major impact.

~ Candace Semigran

Where Do We Go from Here?

Acknowledge the Importance of Love

magine a very young child in a safe, clean, healthy family child care home with a small group of children. Add to that toys; materials that support physical, cognitive, and social growth; and a program of activities that allows all children to explore independently at their own pace. Imagine an experienced, enlightened adult who understands children and keeps the action going.

Now change the picture slightly. Everything is the same, except the caregiver loves this child and all the children she cares for. They delight her and light up her eyes. And she enjoys working in caring partnership with you, the parent. Imagine the possibility of a friendship with this provider that is strong enough to last beyond the child care years.

Every day—every moment—parents in the United States are evaluating child care settings for their children. They have information about safe environments, healthy practices, daily routines, space, and developmentally appropriate materials. They know that they should feel comfortable with the person providing care and that their children should be happy in the child care setting. But they don't know about love.

As a society, we have yet to acknowledge the importance of love in the early years as a critical component of every setting. We

do not promote loving child care as essential, especially for infants and toddlers. But love *is* essential if young children are to develop into curious school-agers, constructive teens, mature and caring adults. This experiment of sharing our children with strangers is still too new to know how to make it work for everyone, but the vision will come. As we add to our collective experience of caring for children beyond kin-related bonds, we will see that loving care is more than a luxury and that warm relationships between caregivers and parents, no matter what the setting, are more than a fringe benefit. We will know beyond a doubt that relationships are the heart of quality care.

The first step is provider education. Providers must recognize that the love they feel for young children is instinctive, natural, and important. Supported by the child care field in this understanding, they will relax their guard and intentionally create new models of care with parents. Compassion will grow as the bonds providers share with children allow them to feel the loss, jealousy, and pain of separation that working parents experience when they leave their children in someone else's care. Parents, feeling understood, will recognize that caregiver-child attachments rest on parental consent. Rather than a threat, they will find comfort in the knowledge that children can love more than one adult.

When we achieve this, *love* will no longer be a dirty word in child care. Children will spend a majority of their waking hours with people who care about them, as well as about one another. Providers will feel supported in their efforts to develop small, caring communities. Working parents will feel release from the guilt and pain of separation. Love will flow in a circle, and affectionate bonds between caregivers, children, and parents will be celebrated for the gift that they are.

Recommendations

 WHERE DO WE GO FROM HERE? In many ways, we are building the road as we go; but as with any important journey, thoughtful, adventurous scouts are already out ahead, exploring the territory and envisioning the potential. The recommendations that follow have been culled from dialogues with these scouts from every economic group and every part of the country. They come from unsolicited comments voiced during workshop sessions, discussions in crowded restaurants, late-night gripe sessions, theoretical explorations at conference roundtables, the "Saturday Search Session on Parent-Provider Relationships" at the 1997 Save the Children National Family Child Care Conference in Atlanta, and from our own intense dialogues with each other as co-authors over the past three years. Born out of crises and longings, frustration and imaginings, these recommendations point the way to a better future for children, for working families, and for the providers who care for that future.

Revise Provider Training ~ As stated before, provider education is most important. From what we've learned through talking to other professionals, we need to revise provider training to do the following:

+ Recognize the natural and healthy inclination of caregivers to bond with children and families. Acknowledge that these attachments are important to all children and essential to the well-being of infants, toddlers, and children in special circumstances or with special needs.

+ Differentiate high-quality infant/toddler care from preschool and school-age care. Clarify that interactions should reflect differences in children's developmental needs.

+ Understand the complementary roles of parents and providers in children's lives. Value the effort to make good matches in child care. Recognize that provider-child attachments rest on parental permission and that children can love more than one adult.

+ Support and strengthen the family unit, recognizing parents as the primary stakeholders in each child's future. Acknowledge the loss working parents experience when they leave their children in someone else's care. Increase understanding and support for cultural differences and individual family needs in the child care setting.

- Help providers balance business and friendship, rather than choose between them.

- Support providers who can work effectively with troubled families, families in crisis, and children at risk. Create systems, services, and special training for providers who do this.

- Support providers who mentor parents with weak parenting skills, teen mothers, single parents, and parents with exceptional needs.

- Strengthen skills in team-building, collaboration, and conflict resolution. Teach providers to focus on problem-solving rather than parent-bashing when they experience typical frustrations.

- Teach providers to cope with grief and loss when child care attachments are ended. Acknowledge that it is natural to grieve when ties of affection are broken.

- Develop avenues for peer mentoring and professional support. Increase opportunities for providers to teach other providers and to serve as advisors when training curriculums are developed.

- Include parents in discussions of child care issues and in shared training opportunities. Invite parents to become active, auxiliary members of professional family child care associations.

Develop Strategies to Teach Parents ~ Parents also need recognition and education. We need to develop strategies that teach parents to do the following:

- Recognize taboos and societal stereotypes that limit child care relationships.

- Choose skilled providers who are gifted in loving, especially to care for infants, toddlers, and children in special situations with special needs. Learn how to make good matches between families and settings for all children in child care.

- Acknowledge the giftedness of providers who are able to love other people's children, and demonstrate a respect for those gifts.

- Understand and cope with normal feelings associated with using child care. Recognize that the family-circle model of care can transform feelings of guilt, jealousy, and loss.

- Understand the complementary roles of parents and providers. Recognize that caregiver-child attachments rest on parental consent, and that children can love more than one adult.

- Give more than money as compensation for high-quality family child care.

- Redesign the family circle to allow room for providers who bond to children in care.

- Understand that children and adults will grieve when child care attachments are broken, and learn how to work through change constructively and with sensitivity.

- Develop skill at conflict resolution. Focus on problem-solving rather than fight-or-flight responses to typical problems.

- Increase parenting skills for all parents and standardize quality child-rearing so that children's needs are met no matter where they spend their waking hours.

Educate Other Professionals ~ Educators, social workers, pediatricians, therapists, consultants, philanthropists, policy makers, child advocates, and others need to revise their thinking and policies. We need to educate these professionals to do the following:

- Recognize provider-child attachments as an indicator of quality child care. Revise taboos and stereotypes that keep parents and providers bound to systems that no longer work for children.

- Advise parents of infants, toddlers, and children with special needs or circumstances to choose caregivers who are skilled in loving children. Create services and systems that enhance caregiver gifts and skills with high-need families.

- Value, protect, and support existing healthy child care attachments. Create systems that allow children to remain in settings where they are loved; ensure quality care for all.

- Distinguish caregivers who offer high-quality child care by offering compensation commensurate with their skills.

◆ Create support programs that teach adults to make good matches, mediate differences, and teach conflict-resolution skills.

◆ Value the work of all adults in our society equally. Move beyond current traditions that devalue the work of those who care for children.

◆ Create parent-provider forums where issues and skills can be explored and improved together. Offer support and insight on ways to redesign the traditional family circle over time to include child care providers.

For Further Reading

Articles

"Becoming Attached." Robert Karen. *Atlantic Monthly*, February 1990.

"Child Care: It's More Than the Sum of Its Tasks." Lynn A. Manfredi/Petitt. *Young Children*, November 1993.

"Children without a Conscience." Tom Keogh. *New Age Journal*, January–February 1993.

"For an Education Based on Relationships: Reggio Emilia." Loris Malaguzzi. *Young Children*, November 1993.

"The Impact of Child Care Policies and Practices on Infant/Toddler Identity Formation." J. Ronald Lally. *Young Children*, November 1995.

"Infants in Day Care: Reflections on Experiences, Expectations and Relationships." Jeree H. Pawl. *Zero to Three: Bulletin of the National Center for Clinical Infant Programs*, February 1990.

"Making Parent Involvement a Reality: Helping Teachers Develop a Relationship with Parents." Susan Brand. *Young Children*, January 1996.

"Meeting the Needs of Infants." Alice Sterling Honig. *Dimensions*, January 1983.

"Mental Health for Babies: What Do Theory and Research Tell Us?" Alice Sterling Honig. *Young Children*, March 1993.

"NAEYC's Code of Ethical Behavior in Early Childhood Education." National Association for the Education of Young Children (NAEYC). *Young Children*, March 1996.

"New Frontiers in Family Child Care: Integrating Children with ADHD." Amy Baker. *Young Children*, July 1993.

"Parents and Teacher-Caregivers: Sources of Tension, Sources of Support." Ellen Galinsky. *Young Children*, March 1988.

"Parents and Teachers: Rivals or Partners?" A five-article section by various authors: M. Coleman, P. Gorham, P. Nason, D. Manning, P. Schindler, C. Sturm, D. Cryer, L. Phillipsen. *Young Children*, July 1997.

"A Puzzle, a Picnic, and a Vision: Family Child Care at Its Best."
Amy C. Baker. *Young Children*, July 1992.

"Quality Wears Many Faces." Lynn A. Manfredi/Petitt.
Windflower's The Garden, Summer 1993.

"A Secure Base for Babies: Applying Attachment Concepts to the Infant
Care Setting." Helen Raikes. *Young Children*, July 1996.

"A Study of Turnover Among Family Day Care Providers."
Margaret K. Nelson. *Children Today*, March–April 1990.

"The Ties That Bind." Colleen Dolan Gomez.
Parents, Baby Care: Birth–3 Months, 1987.

"Who Cares for the Children?" Urie Bronfenner.
The Furture of the Family. Ed. Louise Kapp Howe.
New York: Simon & Schuster, 1972.

Books

The Art of Loving. Erich Fromm. New York: Bantam Books, 1956.

Assessment Profile for Family Day Care: Study Guide. Martha Abbott Shim
and Annette Sibley. Atlanta: Quality Assist, 1992.

The Changing Family. Betty Yorburg. New York: Columbia University
Press, 1973.

Childhood's Future. Richard Louv. New York: Anchor Books, 1990.

*Community Mobilization: Strategies to Support Young Children and
Their Families*. A. Dombro, E. Sazer O'Donnell, E. Galinsky,
S. Gilkeson Melcher, and A. Farber. New York: Families and Work
Institute, 1996.

*The Demand and Supply of Child Care in 1990: Joint Findings from the
National Child Care Survey 1990 and a Profile of Child Care Settings*.
B. Willer, S. L. Hofferth, E. E. Kisker, P. Divine-Hawkins, E. Farquhar,
and F. B. Glanz. Washington, D.C.: National Association for the
Education of Young Children, 1991.

The Earliest Relationship: Parents, Infants and the Drama of Early Attachment.
T. Berry Brazelton and Bertrand G. Cramer. Reading, Mass.: Addison-
Wesley, 1990.

The Erosion of Childhood. Valerie Polakow Suransky. Chicago:
The University of Chicago Press, 1982.

Every Child's Birthright: In Defense of Mothering. Selma Fraiberg. New York:
Basic Books, 1977.

Families: Crisis and Caring. T. Berry Brazelton. New York: Ballantine Books,
1990.

Family Child Care Licensing Study. The Children's Foundation.
Washington, D.C.: The Children's Foundation, 1996.

The Family Child Care Training Study. Ellen Galinsky, Carollee Howes, and
Susan Kontos. New York: Families and Work Institute, 1995.

Family Day Care: Out of the Shadows and Into the Limelight. Susan Kontos.
Washington, D.C.: NAEYC, 1992.

Fatherlove. Richard Louv. New York: Pocket Books, 1993.

First Feelings. Stanley Greenspan. New York: Penguin Books, 1989.

The Four Loves. C. S. Lewis. New York: Harcourt, Brace, Jovanovich, 1960.

Frames of Mind: The Theory of Multiple Intelligences. Howard Gardner.
New York: Basic Books, 1984.

The Future of the Family. Ed. Louise Kapp Howe. New York: Simon &
Schuster, 1972.

Heart Start: The Emotional Foundations of School Readiness, Zero to Three.
National Center for Clinical Infant Programs. Washington, D.C.:
National Center for Clinical Infant Programs, 1992.

High Risk: Children without a Conscience. Ken Magid and
Carole A. McKelvey. New York: Bantam Books, 1989.

Home-Based Child Care: How to Start a Family Child Care Home Series. J.
Brunner, L. Foster, L. Manfredi, J. Marsh, O. Naglish, J. Perreault,
S. Taylor, and N. Wilson-Norris. Athens: University of Georgia
Cooperative Extension Service, 1989.

I and Thou. Martin Buber. New York: Charles Scribner's Sons, 1958.

In a Different Voice. Carol Gilligan. Cambridge, Mass.: Harvard University
Press, 1982.

Kinship and Community: Families in America. Allan J. Lichtman and
Joan R. Challinor. Washington, D.C.: Smithsonian Institute Press, 1979.

Love. Leo Buscaglia. New York: Ballantine Books, 1972.

Loving Someone Else's Child. Angela Elwell Hunt. Wheaton, Ill.:
Tyndale House Publishers, 1992.

The Magic Years. Selma Fraiberg. New York: Charles Scribner's Sons, 1959.

The Monroe-Gaines Parenting Manual: For Parents of Young Children. Lorraine
Monroe and Lonnetta Gaines. New York: Monroe and Gaines, 1991.

Mother-Infant Bonding. Diane E. Eyer. New Haven, Conn.:
Yale University Press, 1992.

*National Child Care Staffing Study Revisited: Four Years in the Life of
Center-Based Child Care.* Marcy Whitebook, Deborah Phillips, and
Carolee Howes. Washington, D.C.: Child Care Employee Project, 1993.

One Minute Self-Esteem. Candace Semigran. New York: Bantam Audio, 1990.

The Ordinary Is Extraordinary. Amy Laura Dombro and Leah Wallach.
New York: Simon & Schuster, 1988.

Parenting Together. Diane Ehrensaft. New York: The Free Press, 1987.

The Politics of a Guaranteed Income. Daniel P. Moynihan. New York:
Vintage Books, 1972.

Power and Emotion in Infant-Toddler Care. Robin Lynn Leavitt. Albany:
State University of New York Press, 1994.

Quality in Family Child Care and Relative Care. Susan Kontos, Carollee
Howes, Marybeth Shim, and Ellen Galinsky. New York:
Teachers College Press, Columbia University Press, 1994.

Ready to Learn: A Mandate for the Nation. Ernest Boyer. Princeton, N.J.:
Carnegie Foundation for the Advancement of Teaching, Princeton
University Press, 1991.

Rethinking the Brain: New Insights into Early Development. Rima Shore.
New York: Families and Work Institute, 1997.

Serving Families. Geoffrey Link and Marjorie Beggs, with Ethel Seiderman.
San Francisco: A Parent Services Project Publication, 1997.

Sharing the Caring. Amy Laura Dombro and Patty Bryan. New York: Simon
& Schuster, 1991.

The Space Between Us: Exploring the Dimensions of Human Relationships.
Ruthellen Josselson. Thousand Oaks, Calif.: Sage Publications, 1992.

Starting Points: Meeting the Needs of Our Youngest Children. Carnegie
Corporation of New York. New York: Carnegie Corporation, 1994.

The State of America's Children 1992: Leave No Child Behind. Children's Defense Fund. Washington, D.C.: Children's Defense Fund, 1992.

The Study of Children in Family Child Care and Relative Care. Ellen Galinsky, Carollee Howes, Susan Kontos, and Marybeth Shim. New York: Families and Work Institute, 1994.

Supporting the Changing Family: A Guide to the Parent-to-Parent Model. High Scope Educational Research Foundation. Ypsilanti, Mich.: High Scope Educational Research Foundation, 1979.

The Tao of Relationships. Ray Grigg. Atlanta: Humanics, 1988.

That's Not What I Meant! Deborah Tannen. New York: Ballantine Books, 1986.

Traits of a Happy Family. Delores Curran. New York: Winston Press, 1983.

Verbal Abuse Survivors Speak Out on Relationships and Recovery. Patricia Evans. Holbrook, Mass.: Adams Media, 1993.

Who Cares? Child Care Teachers and the Quality of Care in America. Marcy Whitebook and Deborah Phillips. Washington, D.C.: Child Care Employee Project, 1990.

Working and Caring. T. Berry Brazelton. Reading, Mass.: Addison-Wesley, 1987.

Yes! You Can Do It! Caring for Infants and Toddlers with Disabilities in Family Child Care. The Children's Foundation (Video and Annotated Resource Directory). Washington, D.C.: The Children's Foundation, 1995.

Publication Information

CC Employee Project
(now known as the National Center for the Early Childhood Workforce)
733 15th Street N.W., Suite 1037
Washington, D.C. 20005
202-737-7700

Children's Defense Fund
25 E Street N.W.
Washington, D.C. 20001
202-628-8787

The Children's Foundation
725 15th Street N.W., Suite 505
Washington, D.C. 20005-2109
202-347-3300

Families and Work Institute
330 Seventh Avenue
New York, NY 10001
212-347-3300

Young Children
National Association for the Education of Young Children (NAEYC)
1509 16th Street N.W.
Washington, D.C. 20036-1426
800-424-2460

Zero-to-Three Bulletin
National Center for Infants, Toddlers, and Families
(Formerly National Center for Clinical Infant Programs)
734 15th Street N.W.
Washington, D.C. 20005
800-899-4301

About the Authors

LYNN A. MANFREDI/PETITT and **AMY C. BAKER** are known nationally in the field of early child care and education as writers, consultants, public speakers, trainers, and practitioners. Both have written articles for *Young Children: The Journal of the National Association for the Education of Young Children* and have regularly presented workshops on a variety of topics at national conferences.

Lynn, a recognized national expert in family child care, worked with parents and children in her own home-based business for more than fifteen years. She has a master's degree in educational leadership from Bank Street College in New York City and has written articles and acted as a contributing editor for a number of early child care and education publications, including Scholastic's *Early Childhood Today* magazine. She served in a variety of roles, including vice president, on the board of the National Association for Family Child Care (NAFCC) from 1988 to 1992. Currently, Lynn is the manager of Save the Children Child Care Support Center's annual National Family Child Care Conference. She lives in Decatur, Georgia, with her daughter, Laura, and a small zoo of pets.

Amy has worked in the field of early child care and education for more than ten years. She has a master's degree in English from the University of Washington in Seattle and has written numerous articles on family child care issues for child care publications, newspapers, and newsletters. She served as a member of the Board of Directors of the Family Child Care Association of New York State for three years and is currently on the advisory board. Amy works for Eastside Family Day Care Satellite in Rochester, New York, where she designs educational programs and teaches and mentors family child care providers who live in low-income urban neighborhoods. She lives with her husband, Ken, and two college-aged children, Johanna and Jesse.

Index

Also From Redleaf Press

For the Love of Children: Daily Affirmations for People Who Care for Children - An empowering book filled with quotes, stories, and affirmations for each day of the year.

Those Mean Nasty Dirty Downright Disgusting but...Invisible Germs - This popular children's book shows the five germ characters that cause illness. Teach children the importance of hand washing. Bilingual English/Spanish.

Those Icky Sticky Smelly Cavity-Causing but...Invisible Germs - This is an imaginative tool to help children develop good toothbrushing habits. Bilingual English/Spanish.

Those Itsy-Bitsy Teeny-Tiny Not-So-Nice Head Lice - Teaches children and adults about how head lice are spread, commonly used methods for getting rid of lice, and ways to prevent the spread and reinfestation of head lice. Bilingual English/Spanish.

Cabin Fever Relievers: Hundreds of Games, Activities, and Crafts for Creative Indoor Fun - Beat the bad weather blahs with this easy-to-use resource. Contains 100s of simple ideas for creative fun.

Room for Loving, Room for Learning: Finding the Space You Need in Your Family Child Care Home - Put together exactly the space that you need for yourself, your family, and the children in your care. Packed with ingenious ideas for better storage and activity areas.

Tips from Tina: Help Around the House—Hundreds of Practical Ideas to Make Family Child Care Easier and More Fun - Shows you room-by-room how to save yourself clean-up time, make routines more fun for kids, and plan ahead for smooth schedules.

The Basic Guide to Family Child Care Record Keeping - Easy-to-follow instructions on how to keep all your family child care business records.

The Business of Family Child Care with Tom Copeland - This introductory video covers the seven most important rules for record keeping, as well as taxes, insurance, contracts, and the Food Program.

Business Receipts for Child Care Services - Handy receipts designed specifically for family child care. Improve your record keeping and your professional image.

Calendar-Keeper - Streamline your record-keeping needs into a single calendar which also contains activities, recipes, menus, and more. Updated yearly.

Calendar-Keeper Cookbook - A great selection of 100 CACFP approved recipes from 20 years of Redleaf's popular *Calendar-Keeper* make this cookbook a hit with providers and the kids in their care.

Family Child Care Contracts and Policies - Learn how to establish and enforce contracts and policies to improve your business.

Family Child Care Tax Workbook - Save time and money and calculate your taxes error free. Includes all new tax information for the year.

The (No Leftovers!) Child Care Cookbook - Contains over 80 kid-tested recipes and 20 complete menus with nutrition information—all CACFP approved. Ideal for larger home-based programs.

Sharing in the Caring - A parent/provider agreement packet that helps you establish good business relationships and enhance your professional image. Also available are *Parent/Provider Policies*, actual forms you can use to create a thorough parent agreement, and *Medical Forms*, actual forms for documenting health and medical information on the children in your care—information that is required by most states.

To order or for more information call
Redleaf Press
800-423-8309